HARLEY-DAVIDSON

ROLLING SCULPTURE

A Pictorial Celebration

By Doug Mitchel

Publications International, Ltd.

All photos by Doug Mitchel, except for those credited to Harley-Davidson Archives.

Preparing and completing a book of this magnitude requires the talents of many skilled individuals. Their work however, would be impossible without the never-ending assistance of the owners of the great machines that fill these pages. Not only do they put up with my constant flow of phone calls, they take time out of their busy schedules to allow me to do my photography at their home or place of business.

I would like to extend a very special thanks to the following:

Dave Kiesow and the talented staff at Illinois Harley-Davidson.

The entire Kersting family at Kersting's Harley-Davidson.

Lee, Dave, and Debbie of Heritage Harley-Davidson fame.

Dale Walksler of the incomparable Wheels Through Time Museum.

Joyce Harlan at Walters Brothers Harley-Davidson.

Marty Rosenblum (owner of the rare 1977 XLCR pictured), Tom Bolfert, and Ray Schlee, keepers of the history at the Harley-Davidson archives in Milwaukee.

Keep the shiny side up,

Doug Mitchel

Sources:
Harley-Davidson Historical Overview 1903-1993
The Big Book of Harley-Davidson, Thomas C. Bolfert
Inside Harley-Davidson, Jerry Hatfield
Antique American Motorcycle Buyer's Guide, Jerry Hatfield
Harley-Davidson: The American Motorcycle, Allan Girdler
Illustrated Harley-Davidson Buyer's Guide, Allan Girdler

Contents

Chapter One

The Early Years. 8

(1903-1928)

Harley-Davidson grows from a backyard enterprise into a major motorcycling force.

Chapter Two

The Flathead Era 26

(1929-1935)

The Great Depression takes its toll on many competitors, but Harley-Davidson weathers the storm.

Chapter Three

The Knucklehead Era 32

(1936-1947)

A new overhead-valve V-Twin gives Harley a leg up on the competition.

Chapter Four

The Panhead Era. 42

(1948-1965)

Harley begins a period of refinement that culminates with a thoroughly modern machine.

Chapter Five
The Shovelhead Era 72
(1966-1984)

Stiff competition from overseas threatens the company's existence, but Harley hangs on with a little help from AMF.

Chapter Six
The Evo Era 100
(1984-1999)

On its own once again, Harley-Davidson comes charging back with fresh engineering wrapped in classic designs.

Chapter Seven
The Twin Cam 88 Era 140
(1999-present)

A new Big Twin is followed by the most revolutionary motorcycle in Harley-Davidson history as the Motor Company approaches its Centennial.

Special Sections:

Foreword

Harley-Davidson motorcycles either have souls or remind us of ours. If you have ever walked into the sacred territory of a Harley owner's garage, you have entered an area that can be compared to a place of worship.

The walls will be decorated with elements of Motor Company memorabilia, replete with banners, posters, photographs of rides taken, motorcycle parts to be installed and those that have been removed, saved as icons, family momentos related to riding Harleys, and tables of drawings, notes, and coveted tools. The drawings and notes are revelations as to how the Harley owner wants to customize his or her bike.

There is a folk art process that takes place once the owners take their bikes off the Harley-Davidson dealer's floor. Willie G. Davidson, Vice President of Styling at Harley-Davidson, calls the motorcycles he designs "rolling sculptures." The Motor Company produces factory fine art and the rider induces folk art upon the vehicle.

It is this highly personalized treatment of the bike that permits its soul, or that of its owner, to be revealed.

There is no other motorcycle in the world that consistently becomes a folk art object (with the subject being the owner's mythological sense of self and machine), for a Harley-Davidson motorcycle is the only two-wheeled vehicle that invariably becomes more than a machine.

The history of the Harley-Davidson Motor Company, which this book expertly celebrates, is a story of machines and those revolutionary folk who ride them; moreover, it is also a tale of cultural significance.

Harley-Davidson folk culture is between-the-lines of this text, just as it exists mysteriously between Harley rider and Harley-Davidson motorcycle.

Martin Jack

Dr. Martin Jack Rosenblum
Historian
Harley-Davidson Motor Company

Some of the photographs in this book are from the Harley-Davidson Motor Company Juneau Avenue Archives, and are identified as such next to the photo.

Introduction

Few could argue that Harley-Davidson is a name recognized—and revered—the world over. The company doesn't just produce motorcycles; it produces an American legend.

Not many businesses survive long enough to celebrate their 100th birthday, and fewer still manage to do so on the strength of their original product. Yet in 2003, Harley-Davidson will celebrate 100 years of building just what it started out to make: distinctly American motorcycles.

With this volume we hope to convey not only the beauty of the machines themselves, but also the legacy contributing to that indefinable element known as the "Harley mystique." While the reasoning behind this phenomenon might be difficult to pin down, the response is not: Harley enthusiasts are among the most devoted followers in the world.

We have divided the book's photographic profiles into seven chapters defined by the company's Big Twin motor generations. Each chapter includes an introduction providing an overview of the products offered during that time along with a look at the period's business climate. Special pages at the back of the book are devoted to the various logos that have graced Harley-Davidsons, as well as the V-twin motors that have powered them. Examples of models and memorabilia are also covered in this section, along with the company's single-cylinder motorcycles and a chronology summarizing the Motor Company's long history.

Scholars have estimated that roughly 300 motorcycle manufacturers set out their shingles across the U.S. in the early part of this century. Fifty years later, the exact figure was much easier to pin down: There was just one. Why Harley-Davidson survived when the others failed is a story these pages can only begin to reveal. We're just glad it did.

The Early Years

At the dawn of the 20th century, motorcycle production was already well underway in Europe but still in its infancy in the U.S. Yet by the time William Harley and brothers Arthur and Walter Davidson pieced together their first motorcycle in 1903, there were already a number of other domestic manufacturers, though most were little more than backyard enterprises. Among them was the Indian Motorcycle Company, founded in 1901, which would later become Harley's biggest competitor.

That first Harley-Davidson differed little from other motorcycles of the time, essentially being a bicycle powered by a simple single-cylinder motor that drove the rear wheel through a leather belt. The normal pedals and chain remained in place so the rider could pedal the bike up to speed to start the motor, as well as lend a little leg power when ascending hills.

Though the 10.2-cubic-inch single-cylinder motor was patterned after an existing design, each part was made by hand. It managed to wheeze out only enough power to propel the machine to a brisk walking pace. A second example with a larger, more powerful motor followed, and it was this machine that formed the basis for the early production versions. Three motorcycles were built that year, and the Harley-Davidson Motor Company was in business.

Production rose to eight units in 1904, then to 16 the following year, reaching 50 in 1906, when the original black finish was joined by Renault Grey. In years to come, the company's quiet motors and grey paint would prompt riders to nickname Harleys the "silent grey fellows."

With the quest for more speed came the need for more power, and Harley-Davidson answered with its now-famous V-twin motor. Introduced at a motorcycle show late in 1907, the first production model was released in 1909 with vacuum-operated intake valves and belt drive—both normal Harley-Davidson practice at the time. Problems surfaced early and the model was pulled after that year, but the V-twin returned in 1911 with mechanically actuated intake-over-exhaust (IOE) valves and a belt tensioning system. With that, a legend was born.

Technology then began advancing at a rapid rate. Harley-Davidson introduced one of the industry's first clutches in 1912, and chain drive became available in 1913. A two-speed rear hub debuted for 1914, followed by a proper three-speed transmission for 1915. Singles were sold alongside V-twins during this period, but they would come and go in future years.

A rather odd 35.6-cubic-inch fore-and-aft flat twin was introduced in mid-1919 but would last only until 1923. Meanwhile, the V-twin, which had grown from 50 cubic inches to 61 for 1912, was joined by a 74-cubic-inch version in 1921—the first of the famed "Seventy-fours." Improvements were made to the V-twin's original IOE design over the years, but by the late '20s they still had exposed valve trains that were messy to run, difficult to maintain, and highly susceptible to wear. Rival Indian had long used a flathead design for its V-twins, and though this configuration was theoretically less efficient, it had been refined to the point where it produced reasonable power while being far easier to service. Harley-Davidson decided it was time to develop its own line of flathead V-twins, and the first examples hit the streets in the closing days of the 1920s.

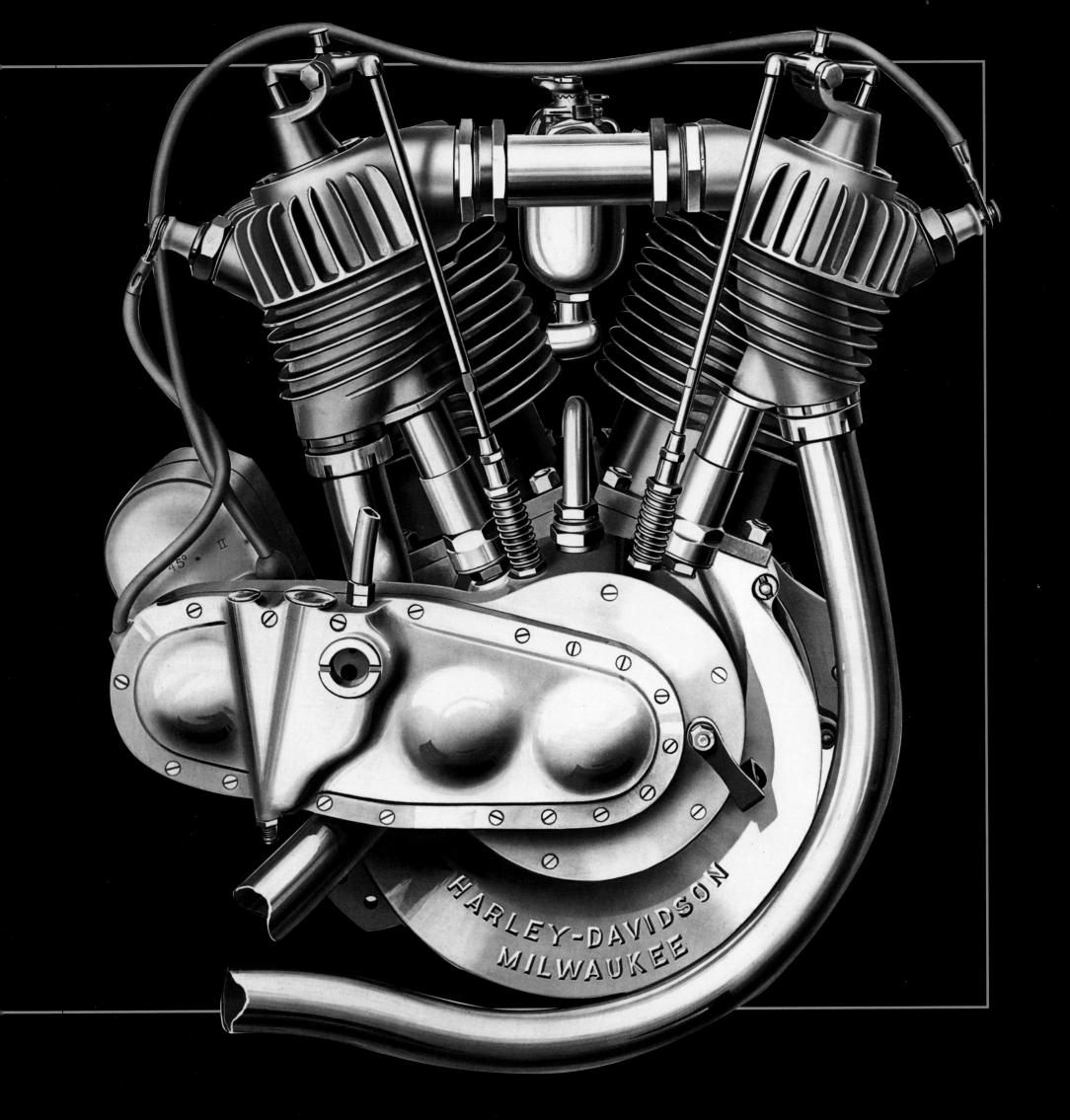

The first motorcycle built by William Harley and brothers Arthur and Walter Davidson took shape in 1902. Power came from a hand-made 10.2-cubic-inch motor based on a DeDion (of France) design, with a vacuum-actuated overhead intake valve and mechanically operated side exhaust valve. Afterward came a stronger machine with a loop-style frame and more powerful 25-cubic-inch motor, and this was the form taken by the first production models in 1903.

The first Harley-Davidson factory (*this page, middle row, left*) was a 10-foot by 15-foot structure located behind the Davidson's family home at 38th and Highland in Milwaukee. It was later expanded, but a larger building was constructed in 1907 at 38th and Chestnut, now known as Juneau—the site of the current headquarters. Shown at right in a circa 1910 photograph are the men whose names were on the building. *Left to right:* Arthur Davidson, who recruited many dealers; Walter Davidson, who brought the company early competition success; William Harley, the engineer of the group; and William Davidson, oldest of the four.

Featured is Harley-Davidson Serial Number One that currently resides in a glass case in the reception area of the Juneau Avenue headquarters.

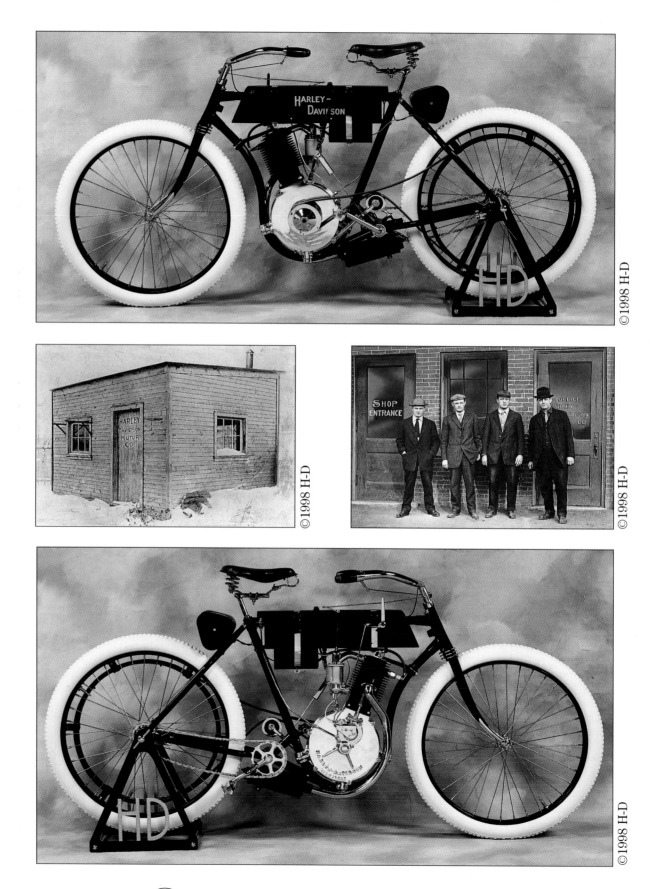

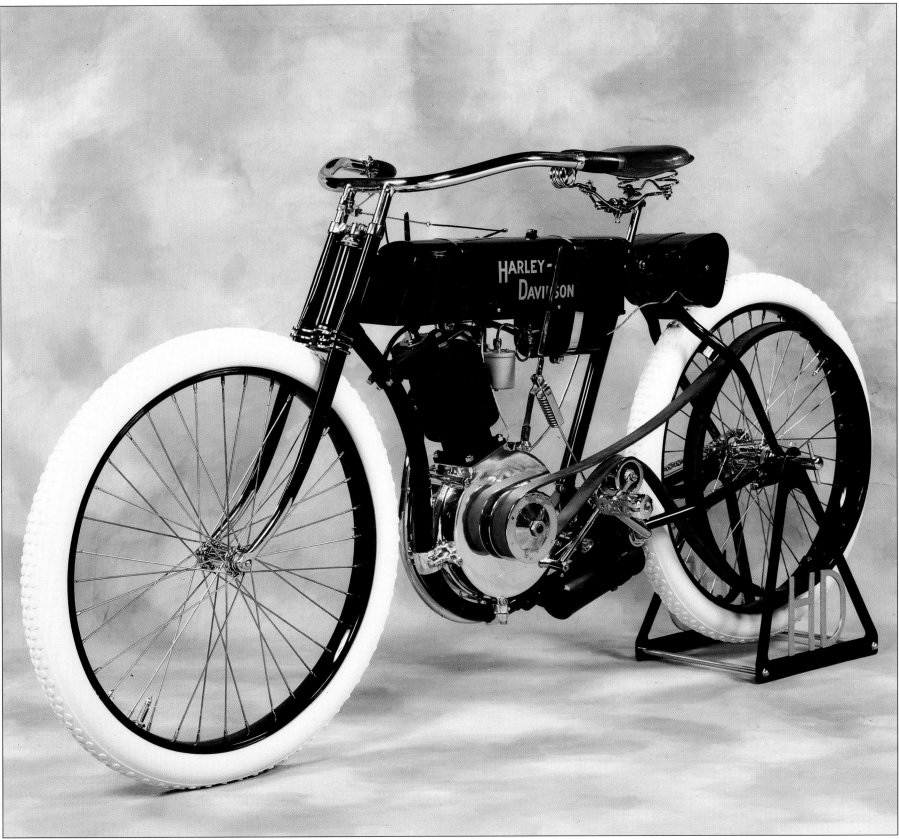

11

Two years after the first Harley-Davidson had chugged its way along the streets of Milwaukee, the motorcycles had changed little in appearance. Power from the 24.74-cubic-inch motor was enough to propel the machine to a reported 25 mph or so. By that time, their numbers had also increased dramatically: Eight of the shiny black machines had been built during 1904, with another sixteen hitting the streets in 1905.

The tall lever along the left side of the fuel tank adjusted tension on the leather drive belt. Since modern control cables had not yet been invented, intricate jointed shafts were used for throttle and other controls.

The motor still used a vacuum-operated overhead intake valve and mechanically actuated side exhaust valve. A trio of batteries supplied juice to the ignition, but there was no on-board method for recharging it. To start the motor, riders would pedal the motorcycle up to speed—not an easy task, as they were not only propelling a heavy bike, but also turning over the motor.

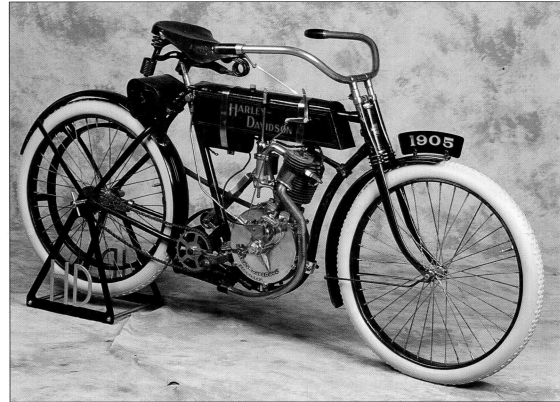

1909 V-Twin

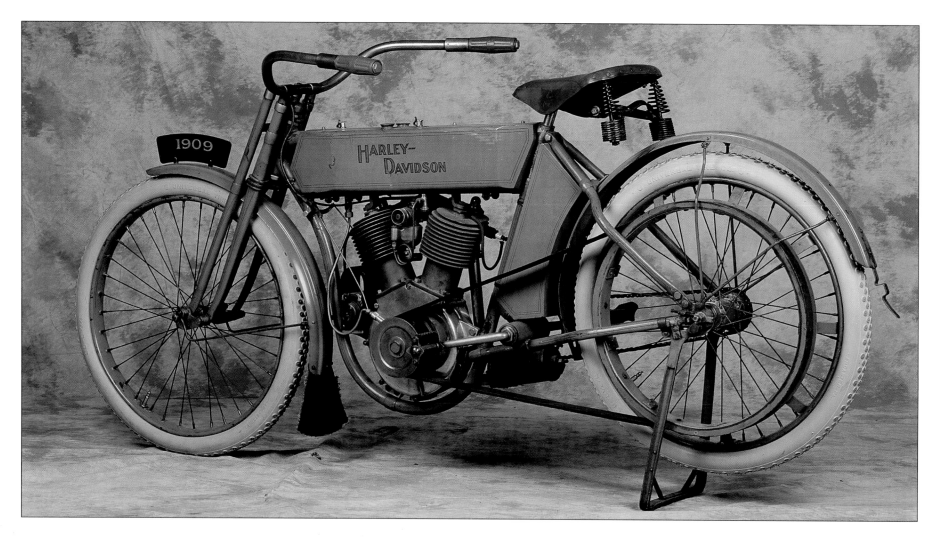

Harley's first production V-twin arrived in 1909. By this time, grey had replaced black as the standard color, and Sager-Cushion front forks were used that allowed a small amount of front wheel travel. Cylinders were the same size as those used for the single, displacement coming out to 49.48 cubic inches. The "V" measured 45 degrees—as have all street Harley V-twins until the V-Rod.

That first V-twin didn't fare well, however, one problem being that the vacuum-operated intake valves did not function correctly. The V-twin was withdrawn from the market for a year, and when it returned for 1911, it had mechanical intake valves. The following year, displacement was increased to 61 cubic inches.

At right is a photo of the Harley-Davidson factory as it appeared in 1908. The building had been constructed two years earlier on a new site at 38th and Chestnut (now Juneau).

1915 11F

After the successful relaunch of the V-twin in 1911, technology progressed at a rapid rate. "Free Wheel Control," Harley's first clutch, appeared in 1912, along with a new frame that lowered the seat and allowed use of the first sprung seat post. Chain final drive replaced the slip-prone belt the following year, and 1914 brought floorboards, a forward-stroke kick starter (using the supplied bicycle pedals), enclosed exhaust-valve springs, and a two-speed rear hub. A three-speed transmission and electric lighting were made available for 1915, though this example carries an "old fashioned" acetylene-powered headlight. The little tyke *(above left)* is straddling a 1913 model.

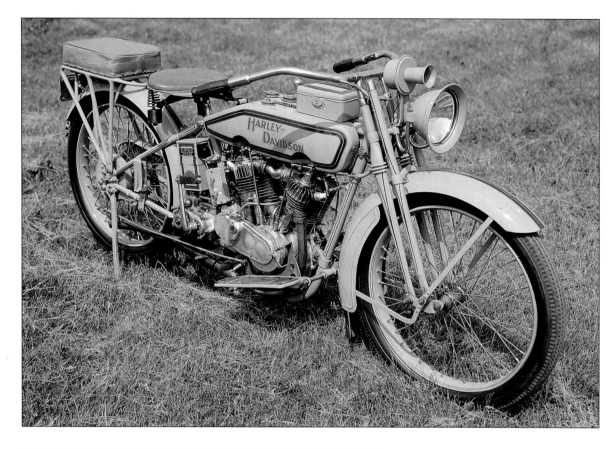

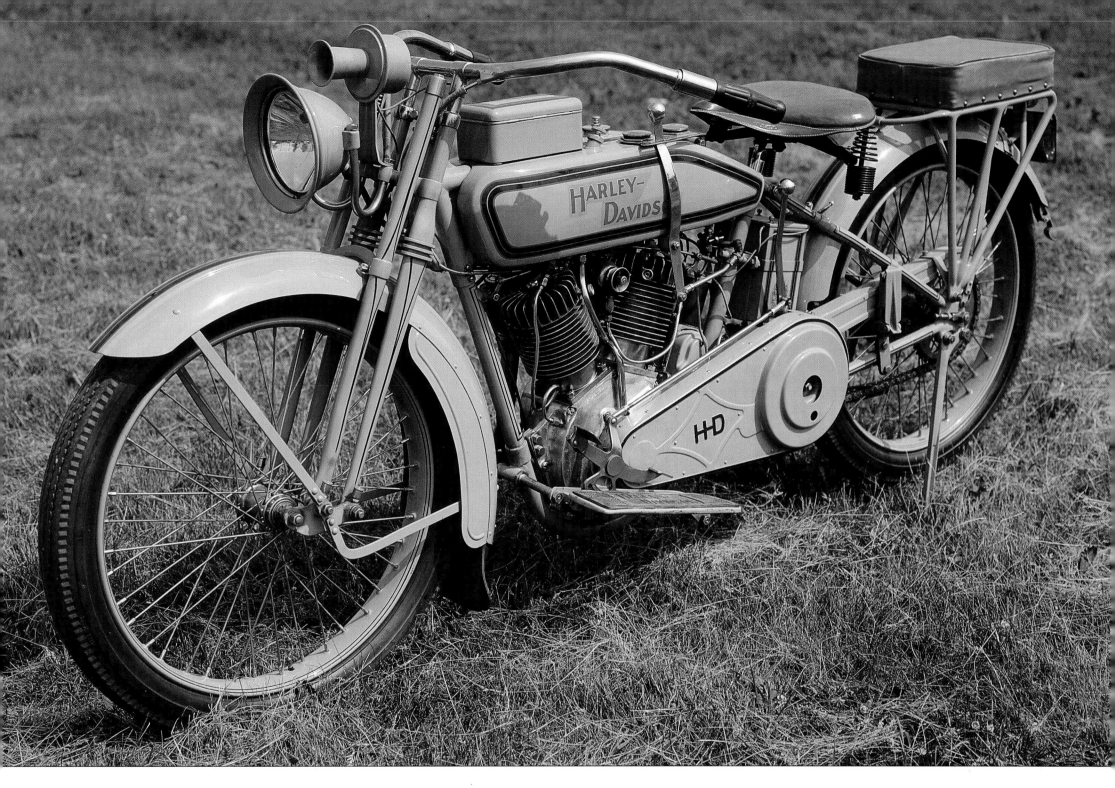

New styling graced the 1916 Harleys, the most notable element being a sleeker fuel tank with rounded contours. Also new was a modern rear-stroke kick lever that finally did away with the bicycle-style pedals fitted to earlier models. These two changes may seem minor in today's light, but were notable steps in the move from motorized bicycles to true motorcycles.

Previously, model designations started with the number of years after 1904 that the machine was built. In 1916, the actual model year was used instead, with the following letter still indicating such features as a generator (J) or magneto (F).

Harley-Davidson's current headquarters building (*opposite page, bottom left*) was begun in 1914. At that time it housed manufacturing as well.

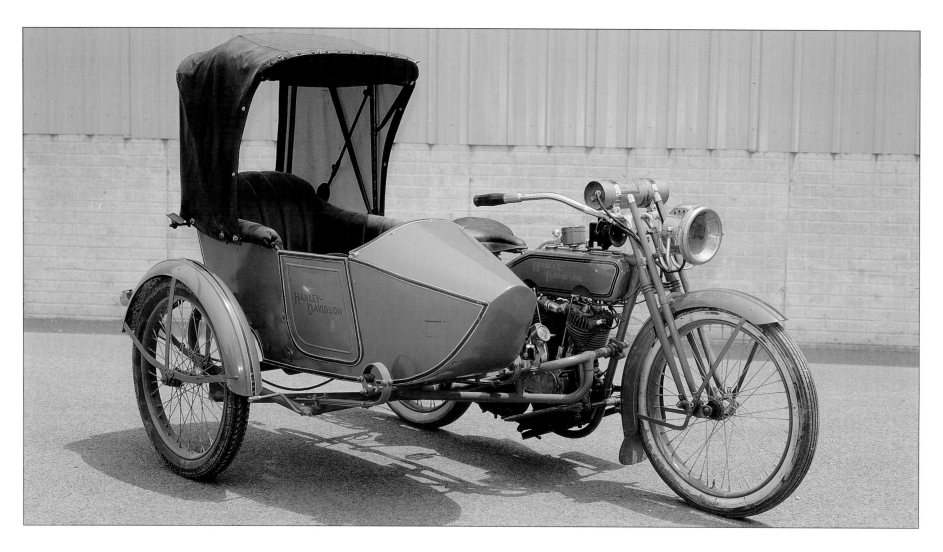

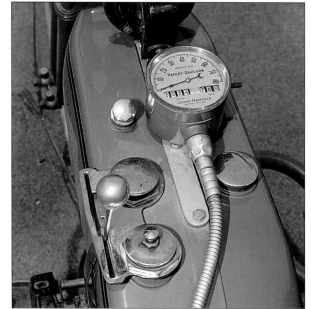

The Model J was Harley's most powerful motorcycle for 1918. As such, it was well suited for use with the matching sidecar, which afforded its occupants far more luxury—and better weather protection—than the motorcycle's rider enjoyed. The staggered shifter gate for the three-speed transmission placed first gear toward the front, with neutral, second, and third to the rear. As it had since 1915, the tank-mounted speedometer was driven by a gear on the rear wheel. Though electric lighting was available, this example is fitted with an acetylene-powered headlight and taillight that were fed from a tank mounted on the handle bars.

Shown opposite page, lower right, is a 1917 Harley as it arrived at a dealership—"some assembly required."

1920 20-J

Harley-Davidson switched to olive paint for its 1917 models. Styling changes were few during those years, the most notable occurring in 1920 when the headlight and horn switched places. V-twins still displaced the same 61 cubic inches (1000-cc) as before, though a 74-cubic-inch (1200-cc) model joined the line for 1921.

Introduced in 1919 was the Sport *(opposite page, lower left)*, a 35.6 cubic-inch twin with horizontally opposed "fore and aft" cylinders. It was intended to compete with Indian's highly successful V-twin Scout, but it failed to win over many customers and was dropped in 1923. *Opposite page, lower right:* A Big Twin (on stand) awaits its motor while a Sport rests in the foreground.

During this same period Harley-Davidson sponsored an extremely successful racing team, which become known as the "wrecking crew" for the way it demolished its opponents. Racing models were devoid of such luxuries as sprung seats and even brakes, and some boasted special overhead-valve engines with two or four valves per cylinder. The 1922 JD racer shown at right is fitted with a conventional F-head engine, and like most Harley competition bikes of the era, carries bolder tank lettering for promotional purposes.

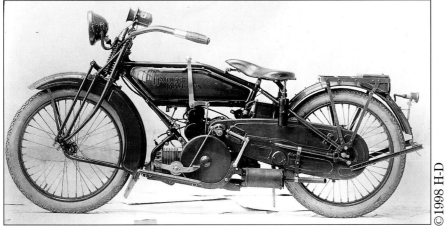

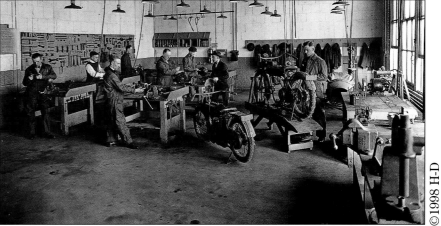

1925 JD

Six Outstanding Facts about Harley-Davidson

HARLEY-DAVIDSON for 1927

Brewster Green replaced olive in 1922, and 1923 models ushered in a hinged rear fender that simplified tire changes. Oddly, olive returned as the standard color in '24, when a box-shaped muffler was fitted—for that year only.

A redesign for 1925 brought a huskier look with a lower frame, more streamlined fuel tank, and smaller-diameter but beefier tires. Seat height dropped by three inches, and the seat itself was a "bucket-type" rather than the flat bicycle-style used previously. Mufflers reverted to a tubular shape. Optional colors became available in 1926 (though they weren't mentioned in any sales literature), and Harley's famous "waste spark" distributorless ignition system debuted for 1927.

Front brakes appeared for 1928, as did high-performance Two Cam variants of the 61- and 74-cubic-inch V-twins (called JH and JDH, respectively). These were among the fastest bikes of the day, capable of hitting 85 mph off the showroom floor. But by this time, F-head engineering had advanced about as far as it could go, and its days were numbered.

The Flathead Era

Harley-Davidson's first flathead V-twin was a 45-cubic-inch unit used in a new bike called the Model D, which was intended to compete with the highly successful Indian Scout. The 45 would prove to be a versatile and long-lived powerplant as it remained in production until 1973. Along the way it served duty not only in street motorcycles, but also in three-wheeled Servi-Cars, military WLAs of the '40s, and WR racing bikes of the '50s. Larger 74- and 80-inch Big Twin flatheads followed, but neither was as reliable or long-lived as the under-stressed 45.

Though flatheads (also known as side-valves) were theoretically less efficient than overhead-valve or even F-head (intake over exhaust) configurations, flatheads were far easier to service and had evolved to the point where power output was competitive—both of which had been proven and capitalized upon by Indian. Factory horsepower charts showed that Harley's flatheads slightly out-produced its similar-sized F-heads, most of the advantage coming (surprisingly) at high rpms. These figures were reflected in on-road performance, where flathead models didn't accelerate quite as quickly due to a sizable increase in weight, but had slightly higher top speeds.

Unfortunately, the flathead models appeared just months before the stock market crash of October 29, 1929. During the depths of the Great Depression that followed, Harley's sales fell to less than a fifth of what they'd been before the crash. But the company managed to keep its head above water while many others were going under, and as the economy began to recover in the mid-'30s, Harley found itself with fewer competitors and an eager clientele.

Prior to the depression, Harley-Davidson focused on its V-twin motorcycles. But the economic slump prompted the company to revive some of its earlier single-cylinder models and even bring out new ones. Also joining the line were industrial engines, special-use motorcycles, and the three-wheeled Servi-Car, which carried its 45-cid flathead V-twin all the way through to its final edition in 1973. Big Twins were not totally forgotten, however, as an 80-cubic-inch version joined the 74-inch model in late 1935.

Despite the flathead's virtues, Harley-Davidson felt a more advanced motor would be needed to keep the company competitive in the coming years. Work began on a new overhead-valve V-twin in 1931, and though it would take five years to come to fruition, the resulting "Knucklehead" would prove a historic advancement.

Yet the flathead design was not ready for retirement. Even after the Knucklehead was introduced in mid-1936, both the 74- and 80-cubic-inch Big Twins remained in the line, as did the 45. Though the 80 would be dropped after 1942 with the 74 following suit after '48, Harley-Davidson continued to offer a smaller-displacement flathead V-twin until the mid-Fifties. And of course the Servi-Car carried a flathead through 1973.

1931 Model D

Harley began switching from F-head to flathead (side valve) V-twins in 1929. First came a new 45-cubic-inch model intended to compete with Indian's highly successful Scout. The following year, the 61- and 74-cubic-inch Big Twins were changed over to a flathead design.

This 1931 Model D is a 45-cid version. Forty-fives look very similar to their bigger brothers, and oftentimes the easiest way to tell them apart is that the Forty-five's drive chain is on the right instead of the left.

Prior to 1933, Harley-Davidson offered custom paint jobs that could be ordered in place of the standard olive. In 1933, the standard finish switched to a choice of two-tone colors with "eagle motif" graphics (right), though olive was still available.

1934 VLD

Color choices widened as Harley-Davidson battled the effects of the Depression; the Seventy-four shown above sports a black with Orlando Orange paint scheme that was a no-charge option. It's also fitted with an optional Buddy Seat, a two-passenger saddle that debuted in 1933 and proved very popular. New styling features included more streamlined fenders and "Airflow" taillight.

Harleys used a hand shift/foot clutch arrangement until 1952, and continued to offer it as an option into the Seventies. Though the shift pattern changed over the years, the clutch was always engaged by pushing down with the toe, and disengaged by pushing down with the heel.

The Knucklehead Era

It wasn't long after the introduction of the flathead V-twins that Harley-Davidson began working on a new overhead-valve version. This is surprising not only because so little time had elapsed since the flathead's debut (the previous IOE design was on the market for over 20 years), but also because the initial decision and engineering work took place during the darkest days of the depression.

Of course, Harley wasn't really breaking any new ground here, as the company had produced overhead-valve singles on and off for many years. But along with the new motor's overhead valves came a recirculating oiling system, and that *was* new to Harley-Davidson. Because of it, the overhead-valve mechanisms were now enclosed—though early models proved far from oil-tight.

Harley's contemporary flathead Big Twins displaced 74 and 80 cubic inches (the latter added in late 1935), but the new motor was sized at only 61 cubic inches. Due to its more efficient overhead-valve design, however, it put out more power. According to factory engineering figures, late F-head and early flathead 74s both put out about 30 horsepower. Later high-compression flatheads were rated at 36 horsepower, but that was still shy of the 40 horsepower claimed for the new overhead-valve motor.

The official name for the overhead-valve V-twin was the "61 OHV," but riders soon dubbed it the "Knucklehead" due to its valve covers, which looked like fists with two knuckles sticking out. Motorcycles powered by the new V-twin were designated the E-Series: E models had lower 6.5:1 compression giving 37 horsepower, while ELs had 7:1 compression and 40 horsepower.

Aside from the OHV motor, the E-Series introduced two more innovations: a four-speed transmission and the now-famous tank-mounted instrument panel. Flathead Big Twins offered the four-speed as an option in 1936, and all V-twins (including the 45) adopted the tank-mounted instrument panel in '37, along with the OHV's recirculating oiling system. With that, designations changed: The flathead Big Twins were now the U-Series rather than the V-Series, and Forty-fives were the W-Series instead of the R-Series.

In 1941, a larger 74-cubic-inch version of the OHV appeared under the F-Series designation. Shortly thereafter the 80-inch flathead was dropped, but the 74 flathead remained available through 1948.

World War II prompted both a military version of the Forty-five and a special horizontally opposed flathead twin with shaft drive that was designed for desert use. The former was called the WLA, and 88,000 were built for use by U.S. troops. The latter XA model didn't fare as well; only 1000 were built, and none saw action overseas.

As it turns out, the revered Knucklehead lasted only a dozen years on the market (and World War II took a chunk out of that), but its influence was far greater than the figure would imply. It formed the basis for all Big Twins produced since, and that's a legacy that can't be ignored—or forgotten.

1936 EL

With speed becoming a greater priority to many riders, Harley introduced the 61 OHV in 1936. The new 61-cubic-inch V-twin boasted overhead valves, and was soon christened the "Knucklehead" by owners due to its valve-cover design, which looked like a fist with two knuckles sticking out. Though the Knucklehead spotted nearly 20 cubic inches to its biggest flathead sibling, it produced more power, and would be the basis for all Big Twin engines for the next sixty-some years.

The Knucklehead-powered model was given the E-Series designation, and carried another element of historical significance: Harley's first tank-mounted instrument panel. Two-tone paint schemes for 1936 ranged from mild (black and red) to wild (maroon and Nile Green, as shown opposite page, top left, on a 74-cubic-inch flathead).

Opposite page, bottom: The first Knucklehead to reach the end of the assembly line is greeted by Harley-Davidson's four founders (left to right) Arthur Davidson, Walter Davidson, William Harley, and William Davidson.

1938 UL

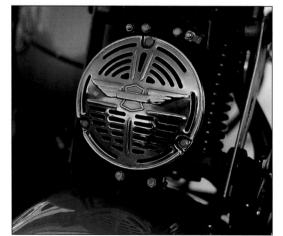

Despite the popularity of the Knucklehead, Harley continued to offer flathead Big Twins. An 80-cubic-inch flathead joined the existing 74 late in the 1935 model year, and for 1937, both gained the recirculating oiling system (replacing "total loss" lubrication) introduced on the Knucklehead. The bikes they powered also adopted the Knucklehead's styling, and these changes prompted new model designations: U for the Seventy-four, UH for the Eighty. High-compression versions of both carried an L as the second letter, so this UL is a high-compression Seventy-four. The Eighty was dropped shortly after the introduction of a 74-cubic-inch Knucklehead in 1941, but the Seventy-four flathead would carry on through 1948.

1942 WLA

Harley-Davidson's military offerings played an important role in U.S. history, as more than 88,000 WLAs were used by allied troops during World War II. Based on Harley's 45-cubic-inch flathead WL, they carried special lighting, racks, and, of course, Olive Drab paint.

Harley-Davidson also built special XA models for the government. These were intended for desert use and mimicked a BMW design with horizontally opposed cylinders and shaft drive. However, only 1000 were produced, and none saw action overseas.

1947 Servi-Car

When introduced for the 1933 model year, the three-wheeled Servi-Car was intended for use by auto repair shops to make house calls. If the mechanic couldn't make the necessary repairs with the tools stored in the cargo box, he could hitch his mount to the rear bumper of the car with a tow bar, and (assuming the car was driveable), take the two of them back to the garage. Likewise, it could also be used to deliver the car when the work was completed.

Over the years, Servi-Cars have been used for all sorts of chores, one of the more common being for parking enforcement. Our featured example was purchased by the Milwaukee Police Department for just that purpose. Note the chalk stick attached to the box behind the seat. Since cars were parked on the right (and therefore the officer would be wielding the stick in his right hand), the throttle is on the left. That necessitated moving the shifter to the right, so this vehicle is set up just the opposite of most.

Servi-Cars were powered by the 45-cubic-inch flathead V-twin and normally fitted with a three-speed transmission with reverse. The '64 model was the first Harley with electric starting. They remained in production through 1973, carrying the old 45 flathead to the end.

The Panhead Era

Harley-Davidson was hard at work on an update of the Knucklehead even during the solemn years of World War II. Engineers revised the valvetrain to incorporate hydraulic lifters that alleviated the need for constant valve adjustment, and the motor ran cooler thanks to revised heads that were now cast out of aluminum. The new heads were capped by redesigned rocker covers that came out looking like upside-down roasting pans, prompting riders to nickname the new motor the "Panhead." It arrived for 1948, and with that, a new era at Harley-Davidson was begun.

Introduced the following year were Hydra-Glide front forks, modern telescopic units that replaced the old leading-link design. Besides doubling the amount of available wheel travel, they also lent a cleaner look to the Big Twins. So monumental was this innovation that the company referred to the bikes themselves as Hydra-Glides—the first time Big Twins were christened with a name rather than just a series designation.

The next few years brought only minor revisions, but 1952 saw the introduction of a hand-clutch/foot-shift option for the Big Twins. Like any change from tradition, this modern arrangement took a while to catch on, but by mid decade, most riders had made the switch. Though hand-shift models were offered by Harley all the way through 1978, annual demand rarely topped 200 units.

Perhaps the biggest news of 1953 didn't have anything to do with styling or mechanical changes, but rather to the motorcycle market itself. After nearly 50 years as Harley's arch-rival, the Indian Motorcycle Company finally closed its doors. Indian hadn't been on firm financial footing since before the war, and the new tide of foreign imports that hit U.S. shores afterward pushed the company over the edge. Yet despite Indian's demise, Harley soon found itself struggling to survive—and for the same reason.

To combat the import onslaught, Harley-Davidson brought out a string of smaller offerings beginning right after the war and continuing on into the mid '70s. First came the S-125 two-stroke single, which remained in the line until the late '50s with only minor changes. Meanwhile, the W-Series 45 was replaced by the K-Series for 1952, the transformation bringing a redesigned flathead V-twin built in unit with the transmission, telescopic forks, and Harley's first civilian rear suspension system. The K's 45-cubic-inch flathead was enlarged to 55 cubic inches for 1954, and three years later the midsize machine evolved into the famed overhead-valve Sportster.

After celebrating its 50th anniversary with some specially trimmed 1954 models, the next big change to the Big Twin line came with the adoption of rear suspension for 1958. With that, the Hydra-Glide became the Duo-Glide, putting Harley's big tourers on the cutting edge of technology . . . well, late 1930s technology, anyway.

Minor alterations were made over the next several years, but it wasn't until 1965 that a major step was taken. In what would turn out to be the venerable Panhead's final season, riders were finally treated to the luxury of electric starting with the introduction of the Electra-Glide. To many, Harley's big touring bike was now "complete," and the Electra-Glide name endures to this day.

1948 **FL**

©1998 H-D

After just 12 years on the market—a mere blink in time by Harley
standards—the famed Knucklehead got a major overhaul. Adding
such features as hydraulic lifters (which eliminated most valve
adjustments) and aluminum heads (which helped the engine run cooler),
the new V-twin was capped with valve covers that looked like upside-down
roasting pans, and soon acquired the nickname "Panhead."

As riders were becoming more concerned with appearances, many parts
were now offered with chrome plating, and accessories (such as the
windshield and fancy seat on the model above) were increasingly popular.

1948 WL and WR

Harley retired the Big Twin flatheads after 1948, so the 45-cubic-inch WL *(opposite page)* was the only flathead remaining in the line after that. Styling was nearly identical to the new Big Twin Panhead models, so the engine was the only way they could be easily differentiated.

The 45 had powered three-wheeled Servi-Cars since their introduction in 1933, and would continue to do so until Servi-Car production ceased in 1973. Few changes were made to the 45 in the more than four decades it was produced, a strong testament to its initial solid design.

Though cherished more for reliability than performance, a good tuner could coax a fair amount of power out of the stout little 45. Racing versions of the WL carried the WR designation *(this page)*, and they were highly competitive machines.

1949 **FL Hydra-Glide**

While the Panhead engine of 1948 was heralded as a major advancement, perhaps even more newsworthy was the introduction of "Hydra-Glide" front forks the following year. Replacing the leading-link springer front ends, these modern hydraulic forks afforded better ride control while providing twice the wheel travel.

So revolutionary were these new forks—at least for Harley—that the motorcycle itself was named after them; EL (61 cubic inch) and FL (74 cubic inch) designations remained, and initial ads referred only to "the Hydra-Glide fork," but later models had "Hydra-Glide" stamped into the headlight backing plate and (in '57) emblazoned on the front fender. This fork design remains in use on some Big Twins today.

1951 Police Special

Harley's police motorcycles not only came with a wide assortment of equipment specific to their duties, but were often available in colors not offered on civilian bikes. Before the war they were usually painted Police Blue, but many postwar models came in Police Silver. Restoration of a police bike is more difficult due to the added equipment, which itself needs to be restored as reproductions are hard to find. The left-side "saddlebag" is actually a two-way radio; a brass fire extinguisher resides on the right.

Not all police bikes were dressed in such a bright uniform. Many were almost devoid of chrome trim, having fork legs, wheels, and primary cases painted black. Harley's first police bike was put in use by the city of Detroit, Michigan, in 1908.

1952 FL Hydra-Glide

The next major advancement for Big Twins came in 1952, when the old hand-shift/foot-clutch arrangement was superseded by a modern foot shift and hand clutch. However, the old setup was still optionally available—and would remain so until the mid-Seventies—as it was still preferred by some riders and police departments.

Never one to turn a deaf ear to its customer's wishes, Harley continued to lavish its bikes with more chrome and polished pieces. Some additional brightwork was made standard, such as polished lower fork legs (which were at first painted black), while accessory packages offered such niceties as chrome fender rails, chrome instrument panel, and chrome front-fender lamp.

Also, the 61-cubic-inch (EL) version of the Panhead was dropped after 1952 due to lack of interest, leaving the 74-cid FL as the only Big Twin.

On the flathead front, the faithful 45-cubic-inch WL was superseded by the Model K, which was entirely redesigned. New features included a foot-shift transmission in unit with a reworked 45-inch flathead V-twin, hydraulic front forks (the WL kept its old springer till the end), and Harley's first rear suspension, a conventional swingarm with dual coil-over shocks.

1954 **FL Hydra-Glide**

A special "50 Years" badge graced Harley-Davidson's 1954 V-twins, because 1904 was considered the start of actual production. However, some 1903 Harleys *were* sold (even though they weren't considered true production models), and it was later decided that subsequent anniversary celebrations would reflect the company's 1903 founding.

Color-matched hand grips and kick-lever pedal were popular dealer accessories of the period. The model below wears two-tone paint (tank and fenders in contrasting colors) and dual exhausts, both of which were factory options.

1955 **FL Hydra-Glide**

New Big Twin features for 1955 included revised cast tank badges boasting a prominent "V" in the background, along with a similar badge on the front fender with "1955" stamped into it. Meanwhile, taillights switched from the old "tombstone" style (which had been in use for nearly a decade) to a new oval design. Also, the existing FL was joined by a performance-oriented FLH with higher compression, hotter cams, and polished ports that resulted in about 10 percent more power. Standard equipment included a Jubilee air trumpet, and a host of optional accessories were available; those fitted to our featured model include body-colored hand grips, chrome luggage rack, chrome engine guard, Buddy Seat with chrome grab rail, chrome fender dressing, and other chrome touches. By this time, chrome trim had become a popular means of dressing up and personalizing one's mount.

When it replaced the W-Series in 1952, the all-new K-Series maintained the 45-cubic-inch engine displacement and side valves of its predecessor. For 1954, however, the engine was enlarged to 55 cubic inches and the model designation changed to KH. In either case, a "K" suffix indicated a sport model with lower handlebars, less chrome trim, and performance-oriented cams.

The KH evolved into the overhead-valve Sportster in 1957, so this 1956 KHK represents the last of its breed—and the last flathead V-twin motorcycle (save for the three-wheel Servi-Car) Harley-Davidson would ever offer.

1957 XL Sportster

After World War II, sporting British middleweights began attracting a growing number of enthusiasts in the U.S. Despite larger displacements, Harley's K and KH flatheads had a hard time keeping up with the more advanced overhead-valve offerings from England, so the company's mid-sized V-twin was itself converted to overhead valves for 1957. This resulted in the famed 883-cc (55-cubic-inch) XL Sportster, which would rule dragstrips for the next decade.

   Like the K-Series that preceded it, the Sportster's transmission was in unit with the engine. (By contrast, Big Twins have always had separate engines and transmissions.) The chassis was carried over virtually unchanged, though a new badge, which was used on all Harley V-twins that year, graced the fuel tank.

1958 **FL Duo-Glide**

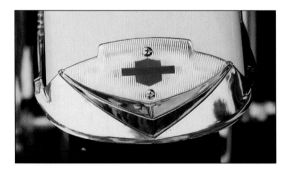

The GLAD RIDE
The GLIDE RIDE
for '58
HARLEY-DAVIDSON MOTORCYCLE CO.
2801 JOHN LODGE
SO. AT GRAND RIVER
PHONE WO. 1-9576

After more than 50 years of hardtail riding, Harley-Davidson treated Big Twin buyers to "The Glide Ride" for 1958. With a conventional swingarm suspension added to the rear, the Hydra-Glide became the Duo-Glide, a transition evidenced not only by the large chrome-covered shocks in back, but also by prominent lettering on the fender in front.

Our featured example is fitted with a host of popular contemporary accessories, including auxiliary driving lights, windshield, engine guard, Buddy Seat with passenger grab bar, luggage rack, saddle bags, and turn signals, items that transformed it into what is popularly known as a "dresser." Note that the rider on the 1958 brochure cover *(above)* is devoid of such "accessories" as gloves, helmet, or even protective glasses.

1959 Police Special

Harley's Big Twins have always been popular with municipalities, most being used for police duty. This example, however, was pressed into duty as a funeral escort. Though it missed out on all the excitement enjoyed by its police-ridden siblings, it has nothing to be ashamed of, as it carries many of the same accessories—siren, red lights, and radio—as the pursuit models. It also wears the special silver paint that was reserved for police bikes, and unlike the civilian models, is not two-toned.

Though a hand-clutch/foot-shift arrangement had been standard since 1952, many police departments opted for the old hand shifter. That way, the foot clutch could be disengaged, allowing the bike to be left in gear with the motor running.

1959 **XLCH** Sportster

A hotter version of the Sportster was introduced in 1958 under the XLCH tag. Intended as a performance-oriented on/off road machine (rumor had it the "C" stood for "Competition," though Harley never said one way or the other), the 1959 XLCH differed from its milder XLH sibling by sporting magneto ignition, high-mounted exhaust pipe, "peanut" fuel tank, "bobbed" rear fender, and semi-knobby tires. Tank badges were also different, being of a design shared by some of Harley's contemporary racing bikes. The

XLCH also debuted the "eyebrow" headlight cover that remains a Sportster trademark to this day.

By contrast, the touring-oriented XLH looked (and was) heavier, with fuller fenders, large headlight nacelle, larger fuel and oil tanks, and low exhaust. Harley-Davidson maintained these two Sportster models through 1979, during which time they proved very successful, both on the racetrack and in the showroom.

1963 **FL Duo-Glide**

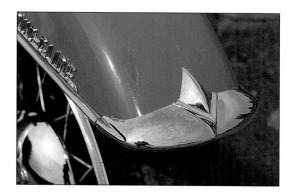

Aside from a new tank badge and paint scheme, the FL didn't change much for '63. However, Harley had tried something different for the '61 models, when the age-old "waste spark" ignition was traded for a more modern—but more complicated—system employing two sets of points and coils. The experiment only lasted through 1964, after which the waste-spark setup returned.

   This is a fairly stripped example of the big FL, as most were fitted with saddlebags and two-passenger Buddy Seat—in addition to the windshield— all being requisites of the well-dressed touring motorcycle.

1965 **FL Electra-Glide**

For the first time since 1958, the FL was treated to something really new: an electric starter. No longer did Harley riders have to struggle to kick over the big 74-cubic-inch V-twin—which had a nasty habit of kicking back. Some riders shunned the idea of an "electric leg," but it was the final step in making the newly named Electra-Glide a true luxury tourer.

Along with the electric starter came a commensurately larger battery, both of which added more weight to a bike that was decidedly plump to begin with. As a result, fully optioned Electra-Glides could now tip the scales at over 800 pounds.

The Shovelhead Era

With the addition of an electric starter and the requisite larger battery, a fully dressed Electra-Glide could amass a good 800 pounds worth of resistance when it came time to move out. Harley-Davidson countered with deeper-breathing cylinder heads for the Big Twin that resulted in a 10-percent increase in rated power. Topping the new heads were valve covers that resembled an inverted shovel, and enthusiasts quickly bequeathed the new motor a fitting nickname. The new "Shovelhead" closely resembled the Sportster's motor—already ten years old by that time—though the smaller V-twin was built in unit with its transmission, whereas the Big Twin, as always, was a separate entity. Few at the time could have guessed the Shovelhead's 18-year reign would prove to be the most turbulent era in Harley's long history.

After going public with its stock in 1965, Harley-Davidson found itself facing ever-stiffer competition from overseas manufacturers. Profits declined, and the company's financial picture looked bleak. Harley began soliciting buy-out and merger offers, and one eventually materialized. In January of 1969, Harley-Davidson merged with sporting-goods manufacturer American Machine and Foundry (AMF).

AMF supplied money to keep Harley-Davidson afloat, and in an attempt to insure a return on its investment, stipulated increased production and expansion of Harley's line of smaller motorcycles. Harley had worked with Italian partner Aermacchi to produce the single-cylinder four-stroke 250-cc Sprint in the early '60s, and now tapped Aermacchi again for a string of even smaller two-stroke machines. These were Harley-Davidsons in name only, and probably harmed the company's image more than they aided the bottom line.

Adding to the problem was that Harley's traditional offerings were losing the almost total domination they had enjoyed in their respective markets. For more than a decade, the Sportster was "King of the Drags," while the big FL had long been the consummate touring machine. By the mid '70s, both were being challenged by less expensive—and more refined—Japanese competitors. Though the Sportster saw an increase in sales during the Seventies, it wasn't as impressive in terms of profits—or quality control. The same could be said for the Big Twins, while the smaller Aermacchi models just plain took a beating.

Yet there were some bright spots. One of the company's most influential products debuted in 1971 as the FX Super Glide. Designed by "Willie G." Davidson, it earned the honor of being the first factory custom. While not an overwhelming success itself, the Super Glide spawned a number of models styled along similar lines, and these eventually became Harley's stock-in-trade.

As the Motor Company soldiered on through the '70s, it became increasingly apparent that hard times lay ahead unless some changes were made. A handful of Harley executives approached AMF with an offer to buy back the company. AMF accepted, and in June 1981, Harley-Davidson was once again in control of its own destiny.

It wasn't going to be an easy trip back to prosperity, but employees, dealers, and owners alike seemed eager to get on the road. And as with any motorcycle journey, the first order of business was to tend to the machinery . . . .

1966 FL Electra-Glide

With increased weight came decreased performance, so it was decided the venerable Panhead, which had served faithfully for 18 years, was due for a freshening. The replacement arrived for 1966, and would itself enjoy a lengthy tenure between the frame rails of Harley's biggest bikes.

Like its predecessors, the new engine was quickly given a nickname based on the shape of its valve covers, which now resembled inverted shovel scoops. Horsepower of the "Shovelhead" rose by less than 10 percent (from an advertised 60 to 65), but with this much mass to move, every little bit helped.

1967 **XLH Sportster**

For 1967, Sportsters offered the electric starter introduced on Big Twins two years earlier. However, it was only available on the "luxury" XLH version; the sportier XLCH stuck with a kick starter, which remained on the XLH as a back-up to the electric leg. As before, the XLH also carried fancier trim, including a large polished headlight nacelle, chromed rear shock covers, and a larger fuel tank.

Harley-Davidson ads in 1967 *(opposite page, bottom right)* boasted of the Sportster's record-setting runs at Bonneville. Though these were highly modified machines, the company could still claim that "Nobody builds a faster stock motorcycle."

1971 FX Super Glide

At a time when many bikes fell victim to the customizer's torch just miles out of the showroom, Harley decided to save people the trouble by creating a custom of its own. The design has been credited to Willie G. Davidson, grandson of one of the founders, who was employed in a styling department that was now under the watchful eye of the company's AMF parent.

Combining the 1200-cc FL engine and frame with the lighter XL (Sportster) front end prompted the FX-1200 designation. In addition, a special stepped seat and "boat-tail" rear fender (patterned after the one used on the previous year's Sportster) were fitted, and the end result was christened the Super Glide.

Our featured bike wears the optional Sparkling America red, white, and blue paint treatment. Early models came only with a kick starter, but an electric starter was offered for 1974, by which time the bike also had a front disc brake.

Though it's a coveted collectible today, the original Super Glide didn't go over all that well. But it introduced the idea of the factory custom, which over the years has been a strong and profitable market segment for Harley-Davidson.

1971 **XLH Sportster**

The boat-tail rear fender design that graced the Super Glide for 1971 originated on the 1970 Sportster. It didn't enjoy universal appeal, but it was offered again for '71 Sportsters as a $60 option. Also optional was the red, white, and blue Sparkling America paint scheme, along with colors such as the Sparkling Turquoise worn by this example. None proved popular enough to warrant a return engagement for '72.

Sportster engines still displaced 883-cc in 1971; for '72, that would be boosted to 1000-cc, a move prompted by the growing number of large-displacement Japanese bikes that were beginning to crowd Harley out of the big-bore sport market.

1973 FL Electra-Glide

Though purchased by AMF in January of 1969, "AMF" didn't begin to appear on Harley badging until 1971. When it did, many owners—not altogether happy about the association—removed the badges and repainted the bike. As a result, relatively few Harleys from the AMF years survive in unmolested condition.

This one did, however. It isn't in pristine shape because it's never even been restored. Save for the inevitable ravages of Father Time, it's an original example—just as it left the showroom—with only 69 miles on the odometer.

1975 XL-1000 and XR-750

L ike their Big Twin brethren, Sportsters of the AMF era often had their appearances altered, so relatively few are found today in their original state. But this gold example *(opposite page)* is an exception, as it has been restored to stock condition.

Government regulations required all motorcycles to have their rear-brake pedal on the right for 1975, so brake and shift arms swapped sides on Sportsters that year (Big Twins already had the brake on the right).

The engine for Harley's successful XR-750 racer *(this page)* was based on that of the Sportster, but it carried dual carbs and high-mounted megaphone exhaust, along with special heads that moved intake ports to the rear of their respective cylinders and exhausts to the front. Though downsized to 750-cc, these engines produced a whopping 90 horsepower, all of which could be set free with just a quarter-turn of the throttle.

1977 **XLCR Sportster**

Harley-Davidson joined the cafe-racer craze of the '70s with the uncharacteristic (for Harley-Davidson) XLCR. Penned by "Willie G." Davidson, the Sportster-based model came only in black with 7-spoke cast wheels, small handlebar fairing, "coffin-shaped" fuel tank, special 2-into-1-into-2 exhaust, rear-set footpegs prompting a "backwards" shift pedal, and a racing-style seat with tail fairing.

Thanks in part to the snake-like exhaust system, the XLCR's 1000-cc V-twin put out more power than the standard Sportster motor, making it one of the quickest street Harleys of the day.

Ads for the XLCR were the first to mention Willie G. by name. The bikes themselves were the only ones built during the AMF years that didn't have "AMF" included in the tank logo; instead, it appeared as a small stick-on label affixed to the side cover. The intent was that owners could easily peel them off—and many did.

Though a classic among collectors today, the XLCR wasn't well received when new, and production lasted only two years (1977 and '78).

1978 **FLHS Electra-Glide**

While the "FLH" nomenclature typically invokes the image of a full-tilt, luggage-laden touring bike, adding the "S" suffix in 1978 brought instead a stripped machine resembling the FLs of old. Adding to the illusion were simple block-lettered tank badges and a large headlight nacelle.

Everything seen on this example is factory equipment, including the twin-stripe whitewall tires and chrome battery cover, as it has never been modified or restored. It is an original bike that has essentially never been ridden.

An 80-cubic-inch motor was introduced for 1978, and eventually became standard on Big Twins. This bike, however, has the 74-cubic-inch version, as the "1200" fender badges attest.

1978 **FXS Low Rider**

Unlike Harley-Davidson's other factory custom for 1977—the less-than-successful XLCR cafe racer—the FXS Low Rider proved an instant hit, quickly becoming the company's top seller. With its low-set handlebars, cast spoke wheels, 2-into-1 header, and ground-hugging stance, this low-slung, dragster-like cruiser was more in tune with the typical Harley-rider's tastes.

A matte-black instrument panel topped the "Fat Bob" fuel tank, which carried decals that echoed the typestyle of Harley's earliest bikes—with the AMF prefix added, of course. Both kick and electric starters were supplied to wake the 74-cubic-inch V-twin.

1978 XL-1000 Sportster

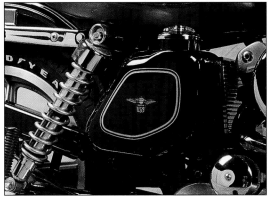

Though Harley-Davidson's 75th anniversary took place while under the ownership of AMF, that certainly didn't prevent the release of special models to herald the occasion.

Sportsters haven't typically been chosen to carry such honors, but along with some specially trimmed Big Twins, Harley built a limited run of celebratory XL-1000s in 1978. Highlighting the jet-black paint were gold striping and gold-tinted cast wheels, while a saddle trimmed in genuine leather added a touch of class. Also on hand were a special 2-into-1 exhaust header and dual front disc brakes. All Sportsters that year boasted a new electronic ignition system to replace the old points and coil setup.

1980 **FXWG Wide Glide**

Harley had introduced the idea of the "factory custom" back in 1971 with the FX Super Glide, but went one step further when it brought out the FXWG Wide Glide in 1980. This one truly had a chopper appearance, with a flamed Fat Bob fuel tank and wide-spaced fork tubes embracing a 21-inch spoked front wheel. A stepped saddle, forward-mounted brake and shift pedals, bucket-style headlight, pull-back handlebars, and bobbed rear fender completed the look.

Powering the Wide Glide was Harley's 80-cubic-inch Big Twin—a fact advertised by the "ham can" air cleaner that substituted for the oval air cleaner used on the 74-inch V-twin.

1981 **Heritage Edition**

One of the first in what would become a series of retro designs, the 1981 Heritage Edition was fitted with a '60s-style headlight nacelle, twin chrome-covered rear shocks, classic Buddy Seat with handrail, and fringed seat and saddle bags. Only the front disc brake and "ham can" air cleaner betrayed its modern vintage. Power came from an 80-cubic-inch V-twin, a displacement that was revived in 1978 after having last been used on a '41 flathead.

Adding to the nostalgic look was an odd olive and orange paint scheme, which may have carried some historical significance but wasn't very popular with buyers, meaning the '81 Heritage is a rare sight today.

1981 **FXB** Sturgis

The FXB Sturgis took its name from the week-long motorcycle event held each summer in Sturgis, South Dakota. The FX designation identified it as a version of the Low Rider; the B indicated that both primary (engine to transmission) and secondary (transmission to rear wheel) drive was via belt rather than conventional chain. Bathed in black, with only small touches of orange and chrome trim, the Sturgis proved to be a very popular model.

The Evo Era

The years immediately after Harley management regained control of the company saw more engineering advancements than any other time since the early Teens. Shortly after the buyback, belt drive— both primary (engine to transmission) and secondary (transmission to rear wheel)—was introduced, as were isolated engine mounts and five-speed transmissions. Not all models had these features at first, but they were there for the asking. The FXRT of 1983 boasted anti-dive forks, and a new XR-1000 Sportster model featured an exotic dual-carb, aluminum-head motor based on the one used for the XR-750 racer.

But it was 1984 that really brought out the goodies. A new Big Twin that Harley called the Evolution V2 arrived featuring aluminum cylinders and revised heads. Still displacing 80 cubic inches, it boasted a higher compression ratio yet was perfectly happy running on regular unleaded gas. Computers were used in the design process, and the end result was a motor that was smoother, quieter, more powerful, and—as time would tell—far more reliable. Per Harley practice, the valve covers were altered in design, this time displaying smooth, billet-like contours that soon had enthusiasts calling it the "Blockhead." Thankfully that name didn't stick, and most now refer to it as the "Evo." Oddly, not all models got the Evo that first year. Shovelheads were built through June 1984, finding a home in—among others—the base Electra Glide.

At midyear came a new wet clutch resulting in lighter lever action and easier shifting. Furthermore, models with primary chains (instead of belts) benefited from the wet clutch because the chain could now be well lubricated without fear of splashing oil on dry clutch plates.

Another innovation was the Softail frame. While it looked much like the hardtail frames of old, the rear section pivoted, extending springs mounted beneath the motor. The design proved very popular and is still in use on many Big Twins today.

The Sportster's V-twin was updated with many of the Evolution's features in 1986, the first time this motor had seen any large-scale revisions since its introduction in 1957. It now came in two sizes measuring 883- and 1100-ccs, the latter growing to 1200-ccs for 1988.

Since the advent of the Evo, Harley-Davidson has produced a host of special models, many of which sold out before hitting the showroom floor. Examples include anniversary editions commemorating the Motor Company's 85th, 90th, and 95th birthdays.

By the late Nineties, Harley-Davidson occupied an enviable position in the business world: Demand for its products far exceeded the available supply, and profits (along with stock prices) were soaring. Because dealers and buyers were both left wanting, the company undertook an expansion program that included the opening of a second production plant in Kansas City during 1998, which helped increase volume from 125,713 in 1997 to more than 168,000 by decade's end.

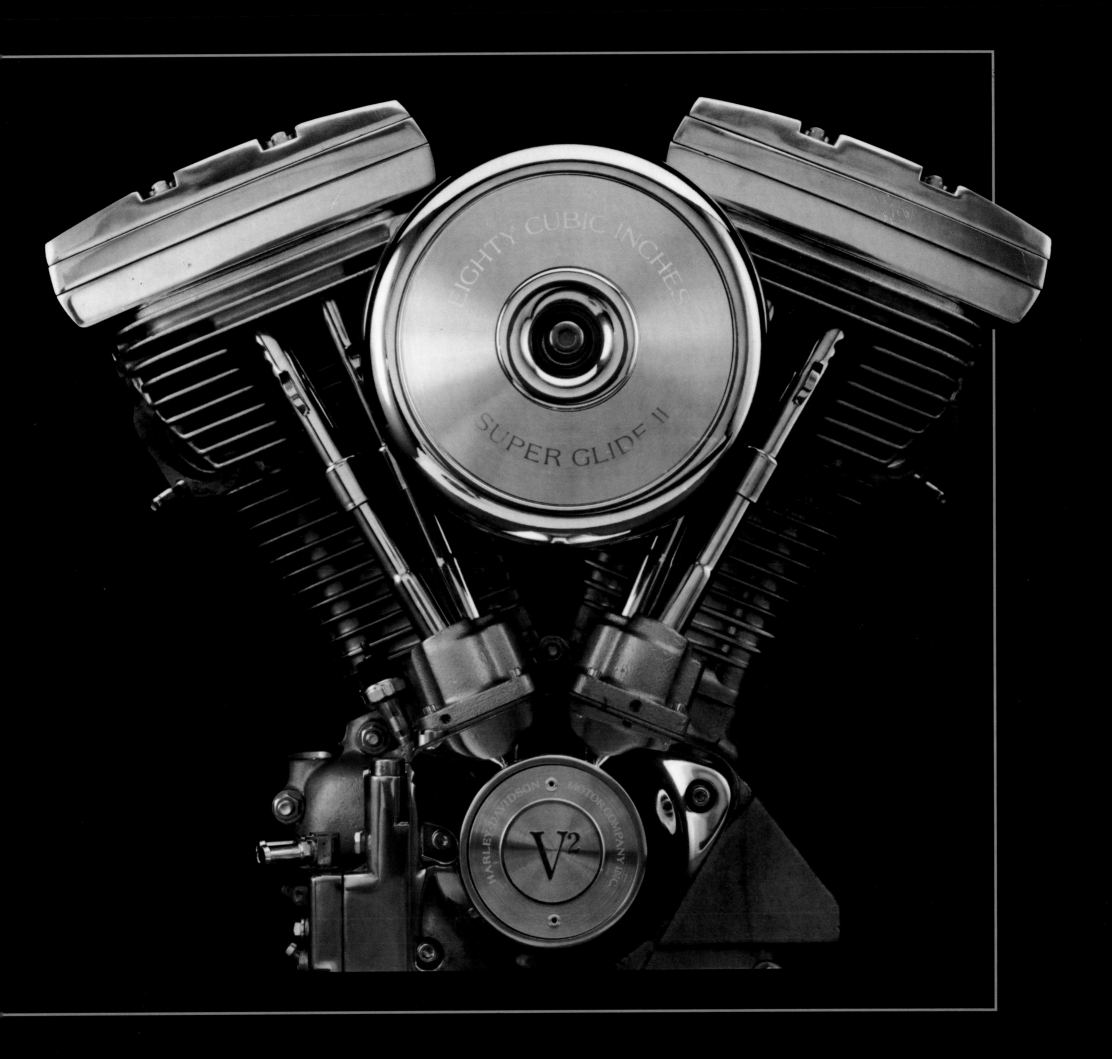

1984 **FXRT**

W hen introduced in 1982, the FXR was heralded as a landmark motorcycle for Harley-Davidson. A stiffer frame with Sportster-style forks provided better handling than any previous Big Twin, while rubber engine mounts and a five-speed transmission resulted in a smoother, quieter highway ride. The 1984 version was among the chosen few to get the new Evolution V2 motor, which further enhanced the FXRT's touring capabilities.

1984 XR-1000 Sportster

Harley's XR-750 racing bike enjoyed such success on the nation's flat tracks that a street version was introduced in 1983 to capitalize on the notoriety. Though based on the stripped-down XLX Sportster, the XR-1000 was fitted with heads similar to those found on the racing version. These brought intake ports entering the rear of both cylinders fed by dual carburetors, and front-exiting exhaust ports emptying into high-mounted dual mufflers. The modifications resulted in an output of nearly 70 horsepower, a figure only dreamed of by other Sportsters, and gave the XR-1000 acceleration unequalled by any

previous street motorcycle Harley had built.

Unfortunately, the race-bred hardware that made the XR-1000 quite fast also made it quite expensive. At nearly $2000 more than the XLX, not enough riders appreciated the difference, and the XR would fade into the sunset after the 1984 model run.

1986 XLH 1100

The Sportster motor introduced in 1957 enjoyed a long life, even by Harley-Davidson's standards. It wasn't until 1986 that it saw any significant changes, but those changes made quite a difference.

Adopting some of the same Evolution technology that had so improved Big Twins two years earlier, 1986 Sportsters got their own version of the Evolution powerplant that was smoother and more reliable than the old design. The new motor now came in two displacements: the original's 883-cc and a larger 1100-cc version. The latter was enlarged to 1200-cc for 1988.

1988 **FXSTS**

Springer forks made a comeback in 1988 after 37 years in hibernation. Advancements in technology had increased their effectiveness, but the look mimicked those that were last used on WL 45-cubic-inch V-twins in 1951, and Big Twins in 1948.

Chosen to showcase the new forks was the 1988 FXSTS. The name said it all: "FX" indicated a Big Twin motor in a cruiser frame; "ST" stood for "Softail," Harley's innovative rear suspension that looked like a hardtail but provided far more cushioning; and "S" denoted the new springer forks, which adopted a forward-mounted shock absorber and were brightly plated in chrome.

Since 1988 marked Harley's 85th anniversary, a trio of bikes carried special graphics and badges to commemorate the occasion. The FXSTS was one of the chosen. Anniversary decals graced the front fender and fuel tank, while our featured model wears accessory cloisonné emblems atop the fuel-filler caps.

1990 **FLSTF Fat Boy**

Harley-Davidson has produced numerous specialty machines over the years, but few have had the impact of the FLSTF Fat Boy that debuted in 1990.

The Fat Boy's simple yet elegant silver paint scheme was enhanced by a matching frame, with subtle yellow highlights being the only idiosyncrasy in the monochromatic theme.

The Fat Boy was alone in its use of solid 16-inch wheels both front and rear, and got a slimmed-down skirted front fender to help differentiate it from other retro-styled Big Twins. It even got its own monogrammed air cleaner.

1991 **FXDB** Sturgis

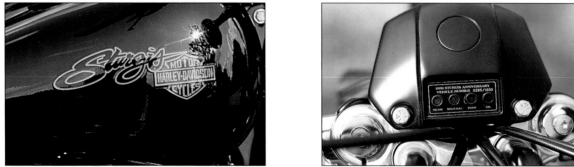

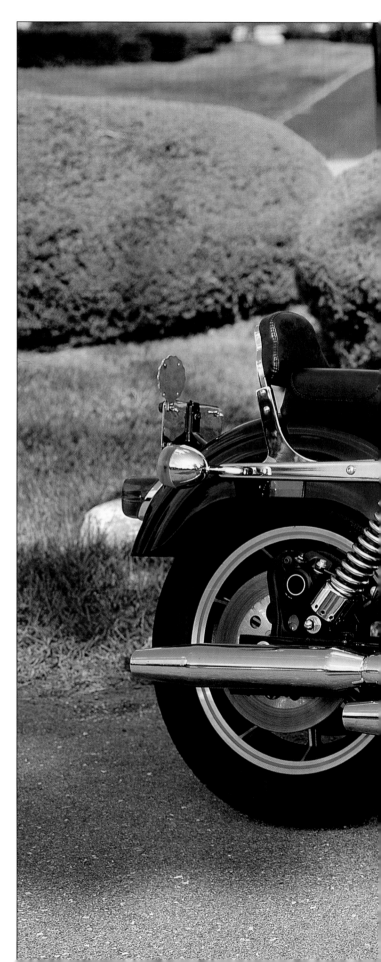

Harley's first Sturgis model of 1980 was powered by a Shovelhead motor; the 1991 edition had the Evolution V-twin (introduced in 1984) nestled in a new Dynaglide chassis. But the theme remained the same, with touches of chrome highlighting acres of black paint with orange accents—Harley's corporate colors.

This Sturgis model celebrated the 50th anniversary of the Black Hills rally held each summer in Sturgis, South Dakota. And like its predecessor, the long, lean Sturgis is a collector's item today.

1992 **FXDB Daytona**

Daytona Beach, Florida, and Sturgis, South Dakota, both host a major motorcycle event each year, and both attract thousands of riders.

In 1991, Harley-Davidson celebrated the 50th anniversary of the Sturgis rally with a specially trimmed FXDB Sturgis model. The following year, a similar tribute was paid to the 50th anniversary of the Daytona meet with the FXDB Daytona.

While the Sturgis wore somber black highlighted with touches of orange, the Daytona was dressed in brighter shades with a more traditional level of chrome trim and boasted Harley's first true pearl paint job. On the tank was a special decal announcing the 50th anniversary as taking place in March of 1991.

Triple disc brakes were bolted to color-matched cast wheels, and highway pegs were mounted to the lower frame.

Production was limited. Only 1700 Daytonas were built, which was not near enough to go around.

1993 **FLSTN**

Among the most collectible of modern Harleys is the 1993 FLSTN, affectionately known as the "Cow Glide." And with its black-and-white paint, whitewall tires, and unique bovine trim (even the tank and saddlebags carried a hint of heifer), it's not difficult to understand why.

Unlike the FX specials of the era, the Cow Glide carried the heavy fork and skirted fenders of the FL models. Built only in 1993, just 2700 copies were produced—far below the level of demand. The FLSTN was offered in different two-tone colors for the next several years, but those lucky enough to get one of the black-and -white '93s were rewarded with an instant classic and a sure-fire future collectible.

1993 FXDWG Wide Glide

In what had become a customary gesture, Harley-Davidson celebrated its 90th anniversary in 1993 with a select group of specially trimmed models. One of those chosen to carry the honors was the FXDWG Wide Glide.

Making its debut in 1980, the Wide Glide got its name from its widely spaced fork tubes. Added to that were a 21-inch spoked front wheel, high pull-back handlebars, forward-mounted foot pegs, bobbed rear fender, and a Fat Bob fuel tank sprayed with flames. Those same features—this time on the new Dyna chassis—marked the '93 Wide Glide save for the flame paint job; in its place, the anniversary edition wore a suit of charcoal and silver—with, of course, anniversary buttons.

1994 FLHTC Ultra Classic Electra Glide

Despite its success with cruisers, Harley-Davidson maintained its presence in the touring market where the Hydra-Glide, Duo-Glide, and Electra Glide had made their marks.

Harley's top tourer for 1994 was the FLHTC Ultra Classic Electra Glide. Fully dressed, it wore a plush two-place saddle, electronic cruise control, cavernous saddlebags and trunk, and a full fairing playing host to an AM/FM/cassette stereo and CB radio—just the ticket for the rider who wanted to heed the call of the wild without forfeiting the comforts of home.

1995 FXSTSB Bad Boy

A new addition to Harley's cruiser line for 1995 was the FXSTSB Bad Boy. Though based on the existing Softail Springer, Bad Boys were cloaked in black from their '40s-style springer fork to their bobbed rear fender, with striping in red, blue, or yellow. Decorating the tank was a jeweled metal badge unique to the Bad Boy. Chrome trim was used sparingly but effectively. Both the slotted rear wheel and spoked front wheel were fitted with drilled brake discs.

The Bad Boy returned for '96 and '97 after which it was discontinued, ensuring its status as a modern collectible.

1997 **FLSTF Fat Boy**

Although the Fat Boy shares components with other Softail models in the Harley-Davidson lineup, it has retained an air of distinction since its introduction in 1990.

Solid wheels, both front and rear, are the most obvious styling cues; until recently, it was the only Harley so equipped. Furthermore, the front fender is unique to this model, and no other at the time shared its "shotgun" exhaust. And the Fat Boy's winged tank emblem—used since the bike's inception—has become a classic.

A polished wraparound nacelle resides behind the seven-inch headlight, adding a touch of the past to the otherwise modern layout. A low seat height and beefy forks give the machine a massive look, and chrome accents abound.

Aside from altered color choices—including two-tone variations—the Fat Boy continued virtually unchanged through its first decade. Nevertheless, it remained one of Harley-Davidson's most popular models during the '90s, and the design was tweaked only slightly when the second generation arrived for the 2000 model year.

1997 **FLSTS Heritage Springer**

Harley-Davidson offered numerous "retro" models during the 1980s and '90s, but none looked as far back into the company's past as the FLSTS Heritage Springer of 1997.

Lovingly nicknamed the "Old Boy", the FLSTS carried design cues dating from the early postwar era. Harleys of the time were equipped with springer front forks, a running light on their heavily valanced front fender, a large chrome horn beneath the headlight, and a "tombstone" taillight—and so was the Old Boy. "Fishtail" mufflers and fringed saddlebags and seat skirts were also popular during that period, and the FLSTS had those, too. What it *didn't* have was a choice of colors: In debut '97, all were white with either red or blue trim.

But like other Harleys of the '90s, the Old Boy boasted modern mechanicals, including an 80-cubic-inch Evolution V-twin and dual disc brakes. In combination with the smooth-riding Softail frame, the FLSTS gave riders the kind of comfort their counterparts of fifty years earlier could only dream about.

1998 **FLHRCI Road King**

Harley-Davidson offered three versions of the Road King for 1998. The standard FLHR could be powered by a carbureted or fuel-injected V-twin, while the Classic came standard with fuel injection.

An assortment of three-dimensional badges set the Classic apart from the base Road King, and the hard leather-covered saddlebags are another visual clue. The wide whitewall tires and slanted exhaust tips continue the division between the two versions of the popular open-road machine. Our featured bike wears Harley's 95th anniversary paint scheme and emblems.

1998 **FLHTCUI**

By combining all the comforts of home with a full complement of electronics, Harley created the ultimate touring rig. The FLHTCUI is the best-equipped Harley ever offered, leaving little to be desired.

In back is a trio of hard luggage capable of swallowing copious quantities of travel gear. Both the rider and passenger are coddled in thickly padded, form-fitting thrones that provide more than adequate comfort on long trips. Not only does the enormous fairing protect the riders from the elements, it houses a host of electronic conveniences.

1998 FLSTS Heritage Springer

The Heritage Springer, introduced in 1997, returned for 1998 unaltered in mechanical specifications. But while the '97 versions came only in white, the '98s were dressed in black. Once again, striping was red or blue, and a '40s-style emblem graced the tank.

From the Springer forks to the wide whitewalls to the fringed saddlebags, the "Old Boy," as it was nicknamed, boasted styling reminiscent of a '40s-vintage bike. The example above carries some optional accessories, such as teardrop front-axle flares. Heritage Springers were also offered in 95th anniversary trim *(opposite page)*.

1998 **FLTRI Road Glide**

New for 1998, the Road Glide harkens back to the FLT of the 1980s. It can be easily differentiated by its half fairing fitted with dual headlamps. Like Harley's other touring models, the speedometer and tachometer reside in a fairing-mounted instrument panel instead of atop the fuel tank. Also included are an AM/FM stereo cassette, voltmeter, oil-pressure gauge, clock, and fuel gauge. Buyers have a choice of feeding the 80-cubic-inch V-twin through a carburetor or fuel-injection unit, the latter being an option that delivers almost 10 percent more torque.

1998 **FXDWG Wide Glide**

First introduced in 1980, the Wide Glide has remained a popular model in the Big Twin line. As in its predecessors, the tall 21-inch spoked front wheel rolls between the namesake wide-set, raked-back forks. Forward foot controls lend a long, lean look to the chassis, and combined with the "ape hanger" handlebars, give the rider a natural laid-back posture. A deeply stepped saddle provides ample comfort for both the rider and passenger, a welcome feature since the 5.2-gallon Fat Bob tank can carry the Wide Glide a long way between fuel stops. This example wears the winged tank emblem and Midnight Red and Champagne Pearl paint of the 95th anniversary models.

1998 **XL-1200C Sportster**

All XL-1200 Customs for 1998 feature a 16-inch slotted wheel in back with a 21-inch spoked wheel up front. Handlebars mounted on risers hover over a lone speedometer, and the bullet-style headlight shuns the "eyebrow" warning-light panel found on other Sportsters.

Mechanically identical to the standard XL-1200C, the 95th anniversary edition wears the special cloisonné tank badges and Midnight Red and Champagne Pearl paint scheme reserved exclusively for anniversary models. Our featured example adds a personal touch with a selection of Harley-Davidson accessories.

The Twin Cam 88 Era

More power, smoother running, quieter operation. Those were the lofty goals set by Harley-Davidson during the development of the Evolution's successor.

And the Evo was a tough act to follow. Since its introduction for 1984, the Evolution V-twin motor had earned an enviable reputation, no doubt being a significant factor in Harley's meteoric rise in popularity during the period. Many felt the company's engineers would be hard pressed to improve upon the Evo's well-established virtues.

But improve upon it they did. Introduced for 1999, the Twin Cam 88 boasted 88 cubic inches (1450 ccs), making it the largest motor Harley-Davidson had ever offered. Increased displacement and freer-breathing intake and exhaust combined for a 10-percent boost in torque. A tighter bore/stroke ratio resulted in smoother running. And a twin-cam valvetrain produced less internal mechanical noise. Yet the engineers weren't finished.

In its debut year, the Twin Cam 88 was fitted only to Big Twins in the Dyna and Touring families; Softails retained the Evo motor. But Softails got their own version of the Twin Cam in 2000—and it was worth the wait.

Unlike Dyna and Touring models, which have their motors carried in rubber mounts (what Harley-Davidson refers to as "vibration isolation-mounted"), Softails have solid-mounted motors. To give them the same smooth operating characteristics as their Dyna and Touring siblings, balance shafts were added to Twin Cam 88s used in Softail models. The result was termed the Twin Cam 88B. And along with their new motor, Softails got a new frame for 2000, as well as slightly—*very* slightly—revised styling that included a larger, one-piece fuel tank on some models. Also new that year was the Softail Deuce, a factory custom with stretched fuel tank and "half moon" rear fender.

Then came a revolution. After years of rumors and speculation, Harley-Davidson unveiled what was unquestionably the most radical motorcycle in its long history: the V-Rod. Arriving for 2002 and equipped with a double overhead-cam, four-valve, liquid-cooled, 60-degree V-twin, the V-Rod stood proud as Harley-Davidson's first "performance custom."

Production continued to climb during these years, with output for 2001 topping 218,700 units. That represented a 30-percent increase from 1999, and was more than double the figure of just seven years earlier.

In June 2003, Harley-Davidson will be celebrating its landmark 100th anniversary. That may still seem a ways off to many of us, but to a company that's been around as long as Harley-Davidson, it's just around the corner. And we can't *wait* to join in *that* celebration.

1999 FLHR Road King Classic

One of Harley-Davidson's most popular models since its introduction in 1994, the Road King adopted a Classic version for 1998 and the new Twin Cam 88 motor for '99.

Road Kings wore the streamlined headlight nacelle first seen on Big Twins in 1960, along with standard hard bags and removable windshield—a combination that made them reminiscent of early "dressers." But these bikes were thoroughly up to date, especially when equipped with the fuel-injected version of Harley's new Twin Cam 88 motor that was standard on Classics. Other "Classic" features included leather-covered bags, wide whitewalls, and distinct tank badges.

2000 **FXSTD Deuce**

From the first day of the Deuce's introduction for model-year 2000, Harley-Davidson has had a tough time keeping up with demand. The combination of custom appearance and contemporary features has made the Deuce a highly desirable creation.

Two of the strongest visual cues are the stretched fuel tank and the straight-cut rear fender. Perhaps not as obvious are the unique "turbine blade" solid rear wheel, graceful tapered fork legs, and small teardrop headlight. Sitting atop the fuel tank is a full-length chrome console housing the traditional lone speedometer, while curved chrome risers bring the cushioned grips closer to the riders' eager hands.

Like all Softails that year, the Duece carried Harley's new Twin Cam 88B motor, the "B" signifying the added balance shafts that provided smoother operation in this solid-mounted application. At first available only in carbureted form, the 88B gained optional fuel injection for 2001.

2001 **FLTR Road Glide**

Riders seeking comfort and convenience with a sportier flair than offered by traditional touring bikes need look no further than the FLTR Road Glide.

A Road Glide is instantly recognizable by its unique frame-mounted fairing incorporating a cut-down windshield and dual headlights. Large-capacity saddle bags, twin exhaust outlets, and full fenders complete the look.

Those wanting something different can fit their FLTR with Screaming Eagle accessories (*opposite page*). In addition to a more powerful 1550-cc version of the 1450-cc Twin Cam 88 V-twin, this example includes floating-rotor brakes, special wheels, chrome-encircled white-faced gauges, and unique Screaming Eagle trim.

2002 **FLSTF Fat Boy**

Harley-Davidson knows enough not to mess with success. So when the Softail line was redesigned for the 2000 model year, it took a sharp eye to tell the "new" versions from the "old."

Most changes were mechanical: The smooth new Twin Cam 88B motor replaced the Evolution V-twin, while the transmission, frame, and suspension were all revised.

Appearance-wise, the Fat Boy carried on much as before, though the fuel tank was larger (5 gallons vs. 4.2), the rear fender had a "flat" lower contour line over the hub, and the exhaust pipes were rerouted to expose more of the motor. But other styling elements remained intact, and the Fat Boy remained one of Harley's most popular models.

2002 FXDL Dyna Lowrider

The FXD lineup contains Harley-Davidson's most affordable Big Twins. Yet despite their basic hardware, these Dyna models sacrifice nothing in the way of style.

Motivated by a vibration-isolated mounted Twin Cam 88 V-twin, the Low Rider earns its name with one of the lowest seat heights of any model in the Harley family. This perch allows even "vertically challenged" riders plenty of comfort and control. The standard Low Rider shown here has accessory saddle bags and windshield, while two-tone paint and spoke wheels are available as factory options.

2002 FXDWG³

Though the FXDWG³ is certainly not Harley-Davidson's *first* "factory custom," it just may be the most radical. Appearance-wise, there is little that has gone undisturbed. A small "bikini" fairing surrounds the headlight, while another mounts to the lower downtubes to direct a cooling breeze to the motor. Air enters a custom filter housing and exits through baloney-cut mufflers. Special five-spoke wheels are fitted, along with a two-position saddle covered in faux animal hide dyed to complement the paint scheme, which itself is accented with flames. Completing the look are custom grips, mirror stalks, and forward-mounted foot controls created in gleaming machined billet. Several engraved insignias call out the proper identification.

The FXDWG³ might not be for everybody, but that's precisely the point; it's aimed at the select few who want something different while keeping their machine "factory stock."

2002 **FXSTB** Night Train

W hen introduced for 1999, the Night Train was a study in basic black. And though it has undergone some subtle changes in the intervening years, the look remains true to its sinister origins.

The first Night Trains were powered by an 80-cubic-inch Evolution V-twin, which gave way to the new Twin Cam 88B for 2000. The following year, Jade Sunglo Pearl was added as a color choice. But all Night Trains share the crinkle-black trim that sets this model apart: The engine and transmission are both cloaked in black, as are traditionally chromed items such as the oil tank, air-filter cover, rear-fender braces, and tank-mounted instrument panel. Yet a few trim pieces remain bright— just enough to be able to spot a Night Train in the dark.

2002 XL-883R Sportster

Harley-Davidson has expanded the Sportster line in recent years to include Custom and Sport models, and has expanded its audience in the process. For 2002, Harley looked to its racing past to find inspiration for the new XL-883R.

Paint and tank decals are fashioned after those of the company's ferocious XR-750 dirt trackers of the Seventies (see 1975 entry), while the satin-black crinkle finish on motor cases, oil tank, battery cover, speedometer, and headlight "eyebrow" lends a business-like appearance. And giving the 883R a performance edge is a gracefully curved exhaust system designed to deliver more horsepower without sacrificing style.

2002 XL-1200C Sportster

Custom versions of the Sportster arrived for 1996 as a way of adding big-Harley styling to the middleweight line. And they've changed little since.

While the powertrain and basic chassis are shared with "standard" Sportsters, Custom models feature a cast 16-inch rear wheel, spoke 21-inch front wheel, drag-style handlebars on chrome risers, and forward-mounted foot controls. A low-mounted speedometer and chrome teardrop headlight sans traditional Sportster "eyebrow" complete the look.

Initially, Customs came only in 1200-cc form; in 1999, an 883-cc version was added, but only the 1200 offers optional two-tone paint.

2002 VRSCA V-Rod

Revolution is more than just the name of Harley-Davidson's new liquid-cooled V-twin; it's the concept behind a whole new breed of motorcycle.

For years, rumors of a "high-tech" Harley circulated like Big Foot sightings at an annual tabloid convention. Liquid cooling? Double overhead cams? Four valves per cylinder? Preposterous! Yet despite the obvious contradiction in design principles, *this* rumor turned out to be true.

Though the V-Rod represents a completely different kind of animal in the Harley-Davidson lineup, its heart comes from an established company source: the racetrack. Harley's VR 1000, which entered the racing scene back in 1994, was powered by a liquid-cooled, double-overhead-cam, 60-degree V-twin very similar to that found in today's radical V-Rod.

Without question, specifications of the Revolution motor are indeed high-tech, yet remain grounded in Harley tradition. A V-twin configuration was a given, though the spread between the cylinders was increased from the usual 45 degrees to a smoother-

running 60 degrees. Both connecting rods still share the same crankshaft journal, but the crank itself is now a stronger one-piece forged unit rather than Harley's usual three-piece design. The traditional overhead-valve layout gives way to more efficient double overhead cams activating four valves per cylinder. Electronic sequential-port fuel injection feeds the hungry pistons, with spark provided by plug-top ignition coils. Liquid cooling—another departure from the Harley norm—promotes more consistent operating temperatures, and the front-mounted radiator carries artfully fashioned scoops on its outside edges to assist airflow. A 2-into-1-into-2 exhaust system culminates in a pair of large slash-cut mufflers.

A vastly oversquare 3.94-inch bore and 2.84-inch stroke (other Harley motors are undersquare) result in a displacement of 69.0 cubic inches, or 1130 ccs—hardly a large motor by Harley standards. Nevertheless, working on lofty 11.3:1 compression, the Revolution belts out an impressive 115 horsepower at 8,250 rpm—more than any other street motorcycle the company has ever produced. A gear primary drive

(rather than the traditional double- or triple-row chain) transfers power to the five-speed transmission through a hydraulically actuated clutch—the first in Harley history.

Designated VRSCA, the V-Rod breaks new ground in other ways as well. While the long, low silhouette is certainly not a departure, the 38-degree fork angle is steeper than that of any other Harley, and contributes to a lengthy 67.5-inch wheelbase—also the greatest of any bike in the line.

A silver perimeter frame wraps around the motor, underlining the anodized aluminum body panels rather than being hidden by them. A special hydroform process is used to produce the extreme curves seen in the upper frame rails, while a lower bolt-on section holds the powertrain.

A twin-filament headlight resides in an ovoid housing that extends up into a pod-like instrument panel carrying a speedometer, tachometer, and fuel gauge. The "fuel tank" isn't a tank at all; it's simply a cover

that hides the downdraft intake system, the real tank being located beneath the seat for a lower center of gravity. Out back, a "clipped" rear fender reminiscent of that used on the Deuce covers a fat 180-section 18-inch tire, versus a 120-section 19-incher in front.

Solid front and rear wheels are fitted to only two Harley-Davidson models: the Fat Boy and the V-Rod. But they are of decidedly different design. Where the Fat Boy's have a "three-piece" look—with the rims riveted to cast disc hubs—the V-Rod's appear to be

turned from a solid block of aluminum. Four-piston calipers grip dual floating rotors in front, a single rotor in the rear. Final drive is by Harley's typical cogged belt.

Even those familiar with the rumors of a high-tech Harley were stunned by the design sophistication of the company's first "performance custom." And the V-Rod stands in evidence that as Harley-Davidson enters its second century, there are many more surprises left to come.

Memorabilia

Long ago, Harley-Davidson began offering non-motorcycle accessories to its avid enthusiasts. Perhaps the first—and still probably the most popular—was a line of clothing. But everything from tiny bottle openers to train sets have been offered since, and some aficionados even keep old dealer signs in their collections. Shown is a sampling of the wide variety of memorabilia (whether or not they started out to be so) that has been produced over the years.

Modeling an early example of Harley-Davidson "memorabilia"—a turtleneck sweater—is this rider of a 1911 single.

Motorcycle trinkets abounded by the Thirties, when this finely engraved combination bottle opener/screwdriver was popular.

Famed Harley-Davidson racer Joe Petrali was said to have coined the phrase "Ride a Winner" that was used on this late-Thirties dealer sign.

Since no Harley yet offered rear suspension in the Forties when this kidney belt with side pockets was offered, it was an eminently useful addition to one's riding apparel.

A late-Fifties Harley matchbook advertisement carries a rather unimaginative tag line. Slogans would get a little better as the years progressed.

This glass mug of the 1980s is adorned with a reproduction of a Harley-Davidson oil-can label—though it's doubtful that holding oil was its intended use.

A ceramic decanter fired in 1988 helped celebrate Harley-Davidson's 85th anniversary.

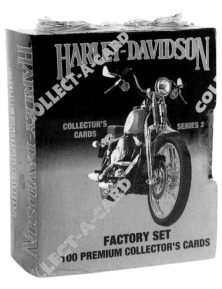

The recent craze in trading cards did not go unnoticed, and several sets of Harley collector cards appeared in the early Nineties.

Road Songs is a two-disc CD set released by Harley-Davidson, complete with leather-bound carrying case.

More of an adult toy is this Harley telephone. The horn honks and headlight flashes when a call is received.

Harley-Davidson licensed this scale-model tractor-trailer rig, which was limited to only 50,000 copies.

Reaching further into the toy market is this Harley train set, a new version of which is released every year.

Twist the handgrip, and this radio/flashlight combination emits a revving sound.

Those seeking to "build" their own Harley piece by piece can do so with this colorful puzzle.

Scale Models

Scale models have long been popular with enthusiasts young and old. The earliest "models" were probably toys made of stamped metal, many featuring wind-up spring motors that propelled them along the floor with a few twists of the wrist. Plastic and diecast models appeared later, with some modern examples exhibiting amazing realism.

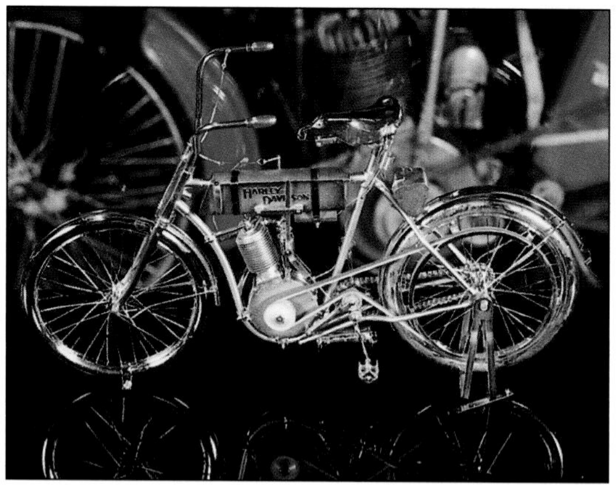

Very early Harley in sterling silver and gold. Released in 1978 by The Heirloom Collectors Guild. Approx. 1/6 scale.

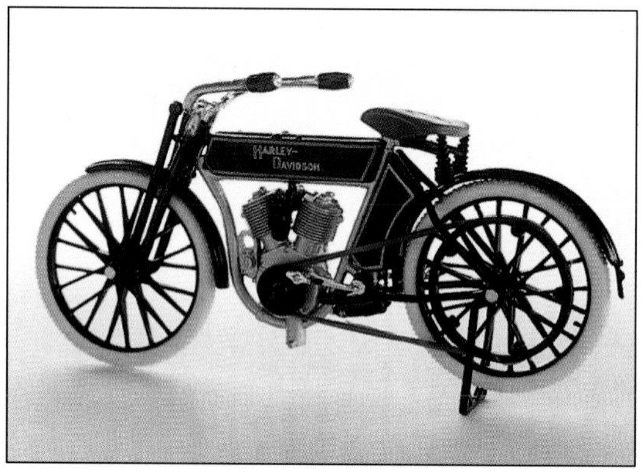

1909 50-cid twin; first of Harley's famous V-twins. Made by Maisto. 1/18 scale.

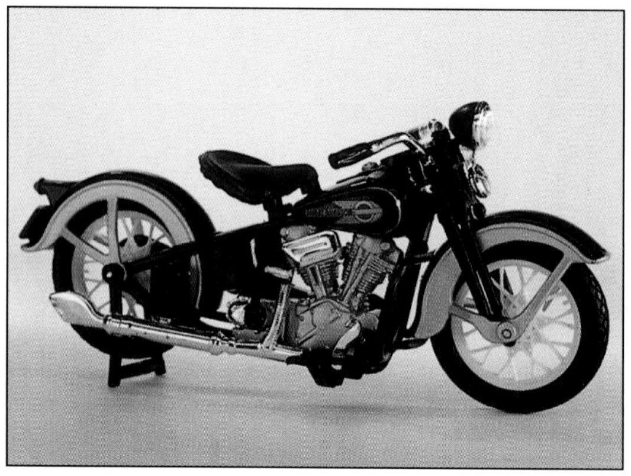

1936 EL—the original "Knucklehead." Made by Maisto. 1/18 scale.

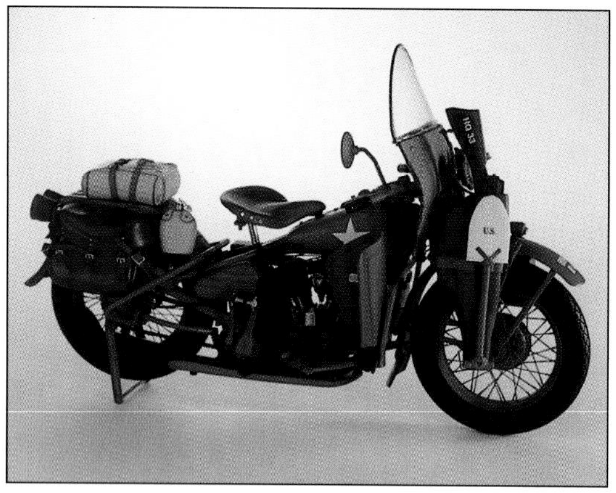

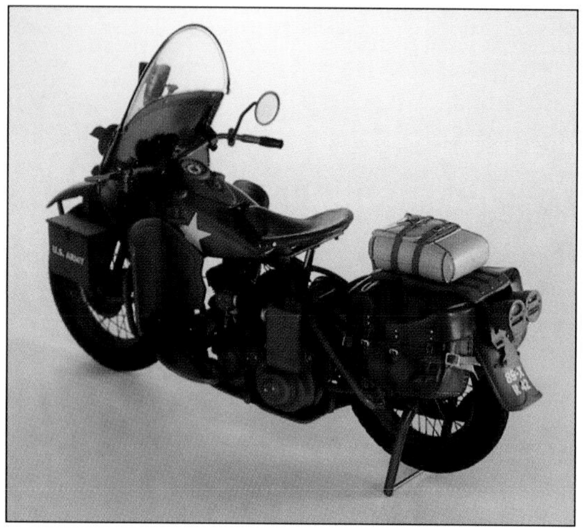

1942 WLA in full military dress with incredible detail. Made by The Franklin Mint. Approx. 1/6 scale.

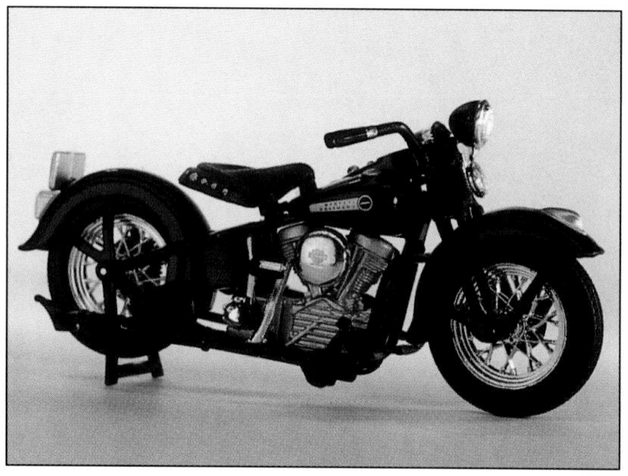

1948 FL. First of the "Panheads." Made by Maisto. 1/18 scale.

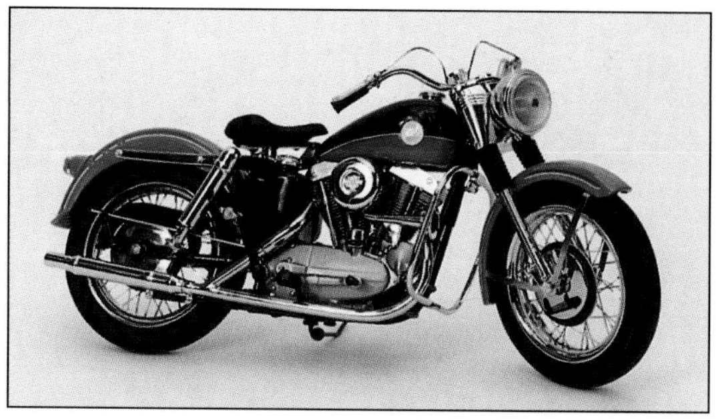

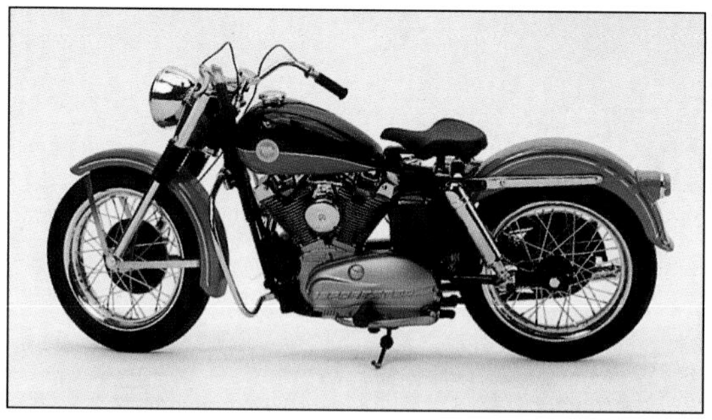

1957 XL Sportster. The one that started the Sportster legacy. Made by The Franklin Mint. Approx. 1/6 scale.

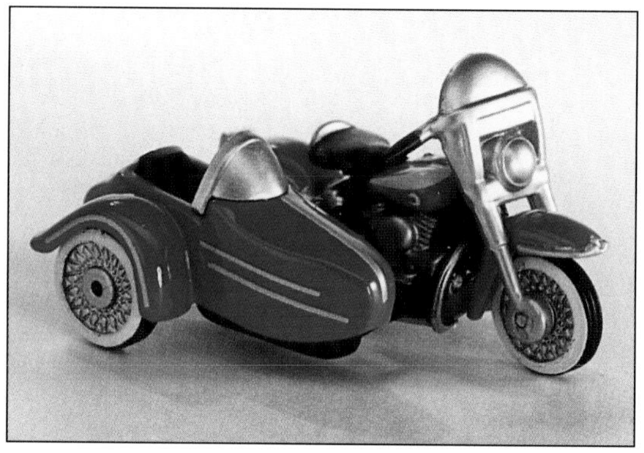

1962 Duo-Glide with sidecar. Made by Hallmark. Tiny: approx. 1/64 scale.

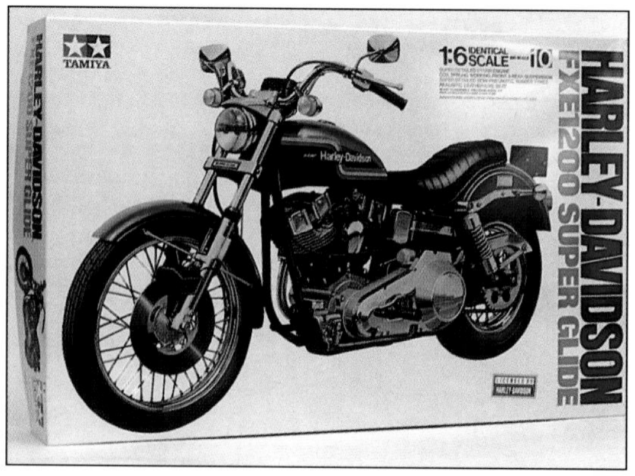

1974 FXE1200 Super Glide. Kit by Tamiya. 1/6 scale.

1997 FLSTS Heritage Springer. Called "Letters to Santa," by Cavanagh. ⅛ scale.

1976 FLH Liberty Edition, offered by Harley to commemorate America's bicentennial. Made by The Franklin Mint. Approx ⅛ scale.

1994 VR1000 marked Harley's return to the racetrack. Offered by Harley-Davidson dealers. ⅛ scale.

2000 FLTR Road Glide. Made by Maisto. ⅟₁₈ scale.

1988 FLHTC—a landmark "retro" model. Made by The Franklin Mint. Approx. ⅛ scale.

1994 FLHRC Road King. Santa on a fitting mount. Called "King of the Road," by Cavanaugh. ⅛ scale.

2000 FXDX Dyna Super Glide Sport. Made by Maisto. ⅟₁₈ scale.

1992 FXDB Daytona. Harley's tribute to the 50th anniversary of the Daytona Beach motorcycle rally. Made by Maisto. ⅟₁₈ scale.

1995 FXSTSB Bad Boy. Perhaps Santa's trying to change his image. Called "Leader of the Pack," by Cavanaugh. ⅛ scale.

2001 XL-1200C. Made by Maisto. ⅟₁₈ scale.

V-Twin Motors

The Harley-Davidson name has always been associated with thundering V-twins. Though different designs in a number of different sizes have been produced over the years, the largest versions have always been referred to as Big Twins—though the same term is also used for the bikes that carried those motors. There have been seven distinct Big Twin design generations, and the company's history is often segmented in accordance with those seven generations—as we have in this book.

Since 1929, Harley has also offered models powered by smaller V-twin motors. Sometimes these smaller models are very difficult to distinguish from their larger brothers, but until recently, one rule had remained constant: Big Twins always carried their final-drive chains (or belts) on the left side of the bike, while the smaller models had them on the right. The exception is the new V-Rod, which has its drive belt on the left.

One more note. While the general rule is that *engines* are gas-powered and *motors* are electric-powered, Harley-Davidson (as well as most motorcycle historians) typically refer to the powerplants as motors—probably because the vehicles have always been called motorcycles, not enginecycles—and we will follow suit.

Big Twins

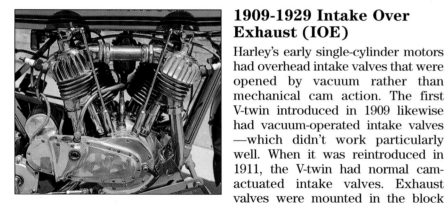

1909-1929 Intake Over Exhaust (IOE)

Harley's early single-cylinder motors had overhead intake valves that were opened by vacuum rather than mechanical cam action. The first V-twin introduced in 1909 likewise had vacuum-operated intake valves —which didn't work particularly well. When it was reintroduced in 1911, the V-twin had normal cam-actuated intake valves. Exhaust valves were mounted in the block (side valve) in all cases. Early V-twins displaced 50 cubic inches; a 61-cubic-inch version was added in 1912.

1930-1948 Flathead (side-valve)

Big Twin flatheads led the line for only six years before being overshadowed by Harley's first overhead-valve V-twin. However, flathead Big Twins remained available through 1948, selling alongside their more modern siblings. Original Big Twin flatheads displaced 74 cubic inches; an 80-inch version was added late in 1935. Though flatheads were theoretically less efficient than the former IOE designs, they had

evolved to the point where they were not only more powerful, but also easier to work on—a major advantage in the days when motors required more maintenance and weren't as reliable as they are today.

1936-1947 Knucklehead

Harley had offered overhead-valve singles in the '20s, but the Knucklehead was the company's first overhead-valve V-twin. The original Knucklehead displaced 61 cubic inches, but a 74-inch version was added for 1941. Though smaller in displacement than concurrent flathead models, the Knucklehead's overhead-valve configuration gave it more power. Introduced on the Knucklehead was a modern recirculating oiling system. Incidentally, "Knucklehead" was not Harley's name for the motor (the factory called it the "61 OHV"). Riders gave it the "Knucklehead" nickname because its valve covers looked like fists with two knuckles sticking out.

1948-1965 Panhead

The Panhead motor was given new aluminum heads that ran cooler than the former cast-iron ones and helped produce more power. It also introduced hydraulic valve lifters, which minimized the tedious task of adjusting valves and also allowed the motor to run more quietly. Like the Knucklehead before it, riders coined the nickname "Panhead" in reference to the motor's valve covers, which now looked like upside-down roasting pans. Initially offered in 61- and 74-cubic-inch sizes, the 61 was dropped after 1952. In its final year, the Panhead was fitted with an electric starter—a real convenience, as Big Twins had become notoriously hard to kick over.

1966-1984 Shovelhead

Redesigned heads gave the Big Twin a bit more power, and the valve covers topping them now looked like upside-down shovel scoops—hence the "Shovelhead" nickname that was once again bestowed by riders. Initially sized at 74 cubic inches, an 80-inch version bowed for 1978 and eventually became the sole offering. Though the new Evolution motor arrived in 1984, some Big Twin models continued to carry a Shovelhead that year.

Big Twins (continued)

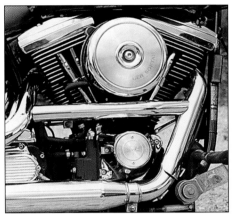

1984-1999 Evolution V2

Harley's Evolution V-twin addressed many of the complaints leveled against the Shovelheads, being smoother, quieter, more powerful, and more reliable. Though some riders early on began referring to the new motor as the "Blockhead" due to its smooth, block-shaped valve covers, the name never stuck and this generation of the 80-cubic-inch Big Twin is usually referred to as the "Evo."

1999-present Twin Cam 88

Though the Evo had amassed a loyal following, the Twin Cam 88 boasted significant improvements in both smoothness and power. Displacing 88 cubic inches, it was the largest motor Harley-Davidson had ever offered. It was followed for 2000 by the Twin Cam 88B, which incorporated balance shafts for even smoother operation in the solid-mounted Softail models.

Smaller Twins

1929-1973 Forty-five Flathead (side valve)

Harley-Davidson's first flathead V-twin was a small 45-cubic-inch motor that preceded its flathead Big Twin brother by a year. It proved to be an extremely reliable unit, and enjoyed the longest life span of any motor in Harley history: Not only was it used in motorcycles for over 20 years, it powered the three-wheel Servi-Car from its introduction for 1933 through its final edition in 1973! It also led an exciting life, being the powerplant of choice for the motorcycles that served the allies in World War II, as well as for racing machines that racked up a long and enviable winning record.

1952-1956 K-Series Flathead

Originally sized at the same 45 cubic inches as its predecessor, the K grew to 55 cubic inches for 1954. It retained a flathead configuration but became the first Harley V-twin to be mated into one unit with its transmission. Like the original Forty-five, it proved to be disarmingly potent in competition, powering winning racers well into the '60s.

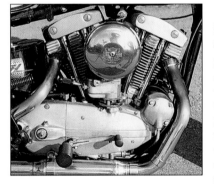

1957-1985 Sportster

The K-Series motor adopted overhead valves in 1957 to become the famed Sportster. Sized at the same 55 cubic inches as the later K-Series motors, it was referred to by its equivalent displacement in cubic centimeters (883-cc) because that's how the motors of its primary competitors were defined. Early Sportsters were among the quickest motorcycles of their day, being the uncontested "King of the Drags" until the late '60s. Displacement grew to 1000-cc for 1972, but even that wasn't enough to put the Sportster back on top in the stoplight grand prix.

1986-present Evolution Sportster

After nearly 30 years, the Sportster's motor finally received a freshening for 1986, taking on the look—and name—of its bigger Evolution brother. For the first time, it was offered in two sizes: the original 883-cc and a new 1100-cc version. The latter would grow to 1200-cc in 1988, which equates to 74 cubic inches—the same displacement as the largest of the pre-1978 overhead-valve Big Twins.

2002-present Revolution

Aptly named, the double overhead-cam, four-valve, liquid-cooled, 60-degree Revolution V-twin broke all the established rules—as did the V-Rod it powered. Based on the motor used in Harley-Davidson's VR1000 road racers, the Revolution displaced just 1130-cc (69 cubic inches), yet produced far more horsepower than any other Harley V-twin in the line.

Classic Tank Logos

In Harley-Davidson's early years, engineering and styling advanced quickly and steadily in the evolution from motorized bicycle to true motorcycle. Conversely, tank graphics changed very little, and it wasn't until the mid '30s that the traditional Harley-Davidson tank lettering gave way to more stylish graphics. After that, new designs came every few years, changing more—and more often—than the motorcycles themselves. As a result, tank graphics are often the best way to determine a restored bike's relative vintage.

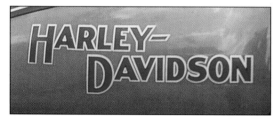

1903-1932
Though colors were altered occasionally, the same basic lettering was used on Harley tanks for over three decades.

1933
The first change to the logo appeared in 1933 when a bird-like scroll surrounded the usual lettering.

1934-1935
Replacing the "bird" motif that lasted only a year was the "flying diamond" design of 1934.

1936-1939
With the new Knucklehead engine came a new tank logo. Though it lasted only through '39, a similar design has appeared on some recent models.

1940-1946
This was Harley's first metal logo (as opposed to a decal). Since World War II interrupted its tenure, relatively few motorcycles carried it. However, a near-copy is worn by the current '40s-retro Old Boy.

1947-1950
This simple design ushered out the Knucklehead and ushered in the Panhead—and the Hydra-Glide.

1951-1954
Arguably among the best of Harley's tank logos, this script design is a classic. In 1954, the same script was used but the underline vanished.

1955-1956
The 1955 design added a background to the script along with a large "V" to capitalize on Harley's famous V-twin motor. It's another classic.

1957-1958
This circular logo was fitted to the first Sportster and the first Duo-Glide. Two-toned paint was used on fuel tanks in 1956, but the schemes were more definitive for '57-'58.

1959-1960
The arrowhead logo was larger and more colorful than its circular predecessor, and seemed to play off the '47-'50 design.

1961-1962
The "gun sight" logo was arguably less attractive than its arrowhead predecessor, and certainly less colorful.

1963-1965

Though the up and down arrows defy explanation, this badge gained notoriety by gracing the first Electra-Glide and the last of the Panheads.

1966-1971

Harley returned to a plain, simple badge for '66 that carried on into the AMF years. It enjoyed a long life by Harley standards of the day.

1972-1976

Harley aficionados didn't particularly like the Motor Company's association with a sporting-goods manufacturer, and the addition of "AMF" to the tank badge didn't help matters any. Most were quickly removed.

Graphics became more diversified at this point, with several different logos appearing in a given year. Following are some examples of the interesting designs that graced Harley-Davidson tanks over the last couple of decades.

1977-1978 FXS Low Rider

The first Low Riders wore graphics that mimicked the lettering used on a 1917 racer—adding the requisite AMF logo, of course.

1982 FXB Sturgis

Finally out from under the AMF corporate umbrella (Harley management bought back the company in 1981), the '82 Sturgis proudly wore the Motor Company's famed "bar and shield" logo—sans AMF addendum.

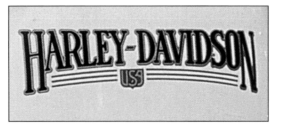

1988 FLSTC

It was only appropriate that decals mimicking designs of old graced the retro-look Softail Custom.

1994 FLHTC

Not only were there numerous different tank designs every year, they were all very attractive—as evidenced by this decal from an Ultra Classic Electra Glide.

1995 FXSTSB

The Bad Boy wore an enameled metal badge reminiscent of a piece of jewelry. It was exclusive to this model and graced the Bad Boy's tank throughout its three-year life span.

1997 FLSTF

The Fat Boy bowed for 1990 with an aviation-themed logo that has since become a classic and continues to this day. A similar design graced the 1993 FLSTN "Cow Glide."

1999 FLHR

While standard Road Kings wore a decal reminiscent of the 1955-56 design, Classic versions got this distinctive badge.

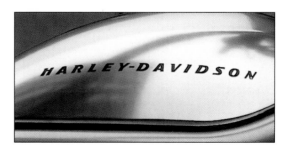

2002 VRSCA

Simple block lettering on anodized aluminum marked the radical V-Rod.

Single-Cylinder Machines

While all early Harley-Davidsons were single-cylinder machines, the Motor Company soon focused on and became famous for its thundering V-twins. Yet over the years, a variety of singles were offered when deemed appropriate, and at times they outsold their larger, more-powerful siblings.

Early single-cylinder models usually resembled their V-twin counterparts. This Model B 21-cid single introduced in the mid 1920s was offered in flathead and overhead-valve configurations, and became known as the "peashooter" due to the sound of its exhaust. It enjoyed a fair amount of competition success.

The Thirty-fifty (30.50 cid) flathead single that debuted in late 1929 in response to the Depression shared its frame with the Forty-five V-twin.

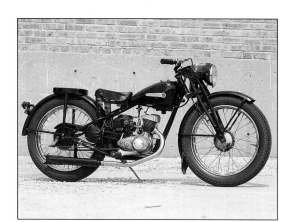

Harley's next foray into singles came after World War II. A small 125-cc two-stroke *(top)* based on a German DKW design was introduced in 1948, becoming the first motorcycle of many a returning veteran. After evolving into the 165-cc Hummer in 1955 and later into 175-cc models in various configurations, it was finally discontinued after 1966.

In 1961, Harley-Davidson joined with Italian partner Aermacchi to introduce the Sprint, a four-stroke single with its 250-cc cylinder pointed straight out the front of the motor. Offered through 1974, Sprints were built in various guises from street bikes to racers in both 250- and 350-cc versions.

The little Topper debuted in 1960 to capitalize on the motor-scooter craze then sweeping the nation. It featured a 165-cc two-stroke engine that was started with a recoil starter (like a lawn mower) and drove through a variable-ratio transmission (like a snowmobile).

Harley's partnership with Aermacchi spawned a number of tiny 50- to 90-cc vehicles starting in 1965 and running into the '70s. These included the M65 *(top)* and Leggero *(middle)* motorbikes along with 65-cc Shortster minibike *(bottom)* and the Z-90 motorbike.

One of Harley's more successful small motorcycles was the 125-cc two-stroke Rapido. It was introduced in 1968 and sold through 1972.

From 1970-74, Harley offered the Baja 100 competition dirt bike. This was followed by the Aermacchi-built MX250 motocrosser, which proved quite competitive, and was produced through 1978.

Replacing the four-stroke Aermacchi singles in the mid Seventies were 175- and 250-cc two-stroke street and scrambler models. These were built through 1978, after which Harley dropped all singles to concentrate on V-twins.

Though not technically within the scope of this book, we'd be remiss in not mentioning two other vehicles to sport the Motor Company's badges. Harley-Davidson golf cars have been around since 1961, and snowmobiles were produced from 1971-75.

Chronology

When a company has been around as long as Harley-Davidson, it's hard to keep track of year-to-year developments. While this is hardly an all-inclusive list, it attempts to highlight the more notable milestones and product advancements in the Motor Company's history.

1903: Three Harley-Davidsons are built

1904: Eight motorcycles are produced

1905: Production increases to 16

1906: Renault Gray joins black as an optional color

1907: Company is incorporated; Walter Davidson is one of three to earn a perfect score in a Chicago-to-Kokomo race; production models get Sager-Cushion front forks

1908: Walter Davidson scores the company's first racing win

1909: V-twin is introduced, but suffers problems and is withdrawn; magneto ignition made optional

1910: Walter Davidson begins to develop a dealer network, a strategy that would later prove invaluable

1911: Modified V-twin returns—for good

1912: V-twin boosted from 50 cid to 61; new frame lowers seat height; Harley's first clutch debuts

1913: Chain drive introduced on some models; all now have mechanically operated intake valves (rather than vacuum-operated)

1914: Step Starter, floorboards, and two-speed rear hub introduced

1915: Three-speed transmission and electric lighting made optional

1916: Fuel tanks get rounded contours; some models get modern kick starter; *The Enthusiast* is first published by Harley-Davidson

1917: Paint switches to Olive Green

1918: Harley-Davidson becomes the world's largest producer of motorcycles

1919: The Sport, with 35-cid horizontally opposed twin, arrives midyear

1921: 74-cid V-twin joins the 61-cid version; 37-cid single added

1922: Brewster Green replaces Olive Green

1923: Hinged rear fender eases tire changes; Sport discontinued

1924: Olive paint returns

1925: Prominent styling changes include teardrop tank, lower frame, "bucket" saddle, and 20-inch (vs. 22-inch) wheels

1926: 21-cid flathead and overhead-valve singles introduced

1927: Big Twins discard distributor ignition for "waste spark" ignition

1928: Front brakes debut on Big Twins; optional and special-order colors are offered; Two Cam models debut

1929: Twin bullet headlights replace single units; 45-cid flathead introduced; 21-cid singles canceled

1930: Big Twin switches to flathead design, is now offered only in 74-cid size; 30.50 single introduced

1931: Single headlight returns; chrome plating appears; Big Twin gets optional reverse gear for sidecar use

1933: Three-wheel Servi-Car introduced with 45-cid V-twin; Harley introduces one of its most popular options, the Buddy Seat; Olive Green is replaced by a variety of standard colors; bird tank graphics appear signaling first real change since 1903

1934: 30.50 single axed

1935: 80-cid flathead V-twin offered late in year

1936: E-Series 61-cid "Knucklehead" overhead-valve V-twin introduced with recirculating lubrication system (replacing "total loss" system) and four-speed transmission; the latter is made optional on flathead V-twins, which continue in the line; tank-mounted speedometer debuts

1937: All flathead V-twins adopt recirculating lubrication system from the 61 OHV; 45s renamed the W-Series; flathead Big Twins become the U-Series; co-founder William A. Davidson dies

1938: 61 OHV gets full valve enclosure to decrease valvetrain wear

1939: Oddly, neutral is moved between second and third in the shift pattern—a change that lasts only one year; aluminum heads made optional on the 45

1940: Aluminum heads are standard on the 80-cid flathead, optional on the 74; all models offer 16-inch wheels in place of 18-inchers; Harley begins building 45-cid WLA for military applications

1941: 74-cid Knucklehead F-Series joins original 61-cid E-Series

1942: Co-founder Walter Davidson dies

1943: Co-founder William S. Harley dies

1944: A total of 88,000 WLAs are built for military use

1945: With the war over, surplus WLAs can be purchased for as little as $25; many are "customized" to hide military origins (and start a trend)

1948: "Panhead" V-twin, with hydraulic lifters and aluminum heads, replaces the Knucklehead; last year for flathead Big Twins, but 45-cid version lives on; S-125 two-stroke single, based on a DKW of Germany design, debuts

1949: Hydra-Glide front suspension replaces leading-link arrangement

1950: Arthur Davidson, last of the original co-founders, dies in car accident

1952: Hand-clutch/foot-shift is standard on Big Twins, though old hand-shift/foot-clutch arrangement is still available; 45-cid K-Series flathead replaces 45-cid W-Series flathead, comes with foot-shift transmission, telescopic forks, rear suspension; old 45 continues to power Servi-Car

1953: Long-time rival Indian Motorcycle Company ceases production; Harley-Davidson is now the only major U.S. motorcycle manufacturer; 61-cid E-Series Big Twin discontinued

1954: 50th Anniversary editions of every model are produced, each trimmed with commemorative badges; K-Series flathead grows from 45 to 55 cid

1957: XL Sportster replaces K-Series with 55-cid (883-cc) overhead-valve V-twin

1958: Big Twin FL finally gets rear suspension in the new Duo-Glide

1959: Performance-oriented Sportster XLCH introduced

1960: Topper scooter is introduced

1961: 250-cc four-stroke single-cylinder Sprint debuts, imported from Harley's Italian partner, Aermacchi; partnership with Aermacchi brings a variety of 50-to-350-cc motorcycles; Big Twin switches to twin-point/twin-coil ignition; H-D golf cars introduced

1964: Servi-Car is first Harley to get electric starter

1965: FL gets an electric starter to become the Electra-Glide, and returns to waste-spark ignition; Harley makes its first public stock offering

1966: "Shovelhead" replaces Panhead Big Twin, brings with it 10 percent more power

1968: 125-cc Rapido joins the line, and remains through 1972

1969: Sporting-goods manufacturer American Machine and Foundry (AMF) buys Harley-Davidson in January

1970: Harley's Sportster-based XR-750 racer is introduced, and racks up an impressive string of victories; Baja 100 dirt bike introduced

1971: FX Super Glide debuts, first in a string of factory-custom bikes; H-D snowmobile introduced

1972: FLs get much-needed front disc brake; Sportster motor boosted from 883- to 1000-cc

1973: Sportsters get front disc brake; last year for Servi-Car; production moves to York, PA, from Milwaukee, where headquarters remain

1974: Aermacchi-built four-stroke singles replaced by 175- and 250-cc two-stroke models

1975: Per government mandate, Sportster switches to left-side shift (Big Twins had always had it); production moves to York, PA

1976: Celebrating America's bicentennial, Harley introduces five "Liberty Edition" models

1977: MX-250 motocross bike debuts; cafe-racer XLCR and custom FXS Low Rider introduced; Big Twin sidecar fans lose the three-speed plus reverse transmission

1978: 80-cid version of Shovelhead is introduced on Electra-Glide, and is later adopted by all Big Twins; Harley builds 75th anniversary Sportsters and Big Twins

1981: Harley management buys the Motor Company back from AMF

1982: FXR appears with five-speed transmission and rubber-mounted drivetrain

1983: Sportster XR-1000 introduced; Harley Owners Group (H.O.G.) formed; government orders tariff on imports over 700-cc

1984: Evolution V2 motor introduced on some Big Twins; Shovelhead powers others for one more year; Softail frame debuts

1986: Sportsters gain their own version of the Evolution motor, now in 883-and 1100-cc sizes; Heritage Softail debuts

1987: Harley-Davidson stock goes public in July; 30th anniversary Sportster offered

1988: Harley-Davidson celebrates its 85th birthday with three specially trimmed models; springer forks make a comeback on the custom FXSTS

1990: Fat Boy debuts

1993: The Motor Company's 90th anniversary is celebrated with specially trimmed models

1995: Fuel injection introduced; production tops 100,000

1997: Heritage Springer debuts

1998: Harley-Davidson offers special 95th anniversary trim on several models; new plant devoted to Sportster production opens in Kansas City

1999: Twin Cam 88 motor introduced on Dyna and Touring Big Twins; Softails retain Evo; Night Train debuts

2000: Softails get new balance-shaft-equipped Twin Cam 88B; Deuce is introduced

2001: Production tops 218,000

2002: Revolutionary V-Rod unveiled

Index